The
INFORMED FED

A Survival guide to your
employee benefits

TRACY MITCHELL

THE INFORMED FED
A Survival guide to your employee benefits

Address all inquiries to:
Tracy Mitchell
1531 E. Bradford Parkway Suite 303-B
Springfield, MO 65804
Phone: (417) 429-0331
www.retirementexpertmissouri.com
www.federalemp.com

ISBN: 978-1-482344-35-6

Editor: Beverly Holloran
Interior Layout: Fusion Creative Works, www.fusioncw.com

Printed in the United States of America

For additional copies call 1-417-429-0331

Author's Note

A prudent question is one-half of wisdom.
– Francis Bacon

We have heard it before; there are no stupid questions. When it comes to getting the most from your federal benefits, this axiom could not be more true. As you read the material and have questions, write them down for review later. You can contact me to expand on these questions which will increase your understanding at a much more rapid rate. I have designed this book to be a road map of information.

How you interpret and ultimately put this knowledge to work is entirely up to you. As you approach your study, utilize a proactive stance. This will position your thought processes in a manner that will keep you thinking and excited about what's around the next turn.

Think about how much better you will feel about yourself, your career and future retirement when you know that you have the knowledge to get the most out of your valuable benefits.

Help your fellow employees by sharing your newfound understanding and confidence.

Federal Employee Benefits

Individual situations will vary and your particular benefits can change; therefore, this information should be relied upon when coordinated with individual professional advice.

You don't need a PhD to understand your benefits. With *The Informed Fed* you will gain a better understanding by simply taking the time to review the enclosed material.

Contents

INTRODUCTION

Education is the Key!

If you think education is expensive – try ignorance.
–Derek Bok

Most would agree that we live in a much different world than we did just 10 to 15 years ago. I can remember my first cell phone. I was required to go to the provider and have it installed in my car. This thing was the size of a brick; what a marvel of technology, I thought at the time! Now, my cell phone fits in my pocket, will access the internet, play my favorite music, has GPS functions and holds my calendar. It even talks back to me and tells me where the nearest point of interest is located.

It is an age of expanding and increasing knowledge at our finger tips, and yet most people do not know how to perform the simplest financial task of balancing their checkbook! It is also an age of increasing uncertainty. Who would have ever thought that our entire financial system would be brought to its knees because of a little known obscure lending practice known as the "Subprime Mortgage"? There are approximately 78 million Americans born between 1946 and 1964 that are retiring at a rate of 10,000 per day. The first one retired in January 2008. We call these folks "Baby Boomers".

It is predicted that they will cause additional burdens upon our financial and entitlement system due to the massive numbers being placed upon the social security and Medicare rolls. You may read that and think to yourself; thanks for the uplifting start to your book! Well, it's not all bad and I think we certainly need to keep things in perspective. In light of all the bad press, there is a silver lining.

I was prompted to write this book because of the number of times I would conduct a review of benefits for an employee and discover that they had no idea how their benefits were structured or what options they had chosen and the impact it would have on future earnings. They simply completed the new employee forms by making a few selections and then forgot about it. They would meet with an advisor in the latter years of their career only to find out that they should have been consulting with one throughout their career. I can't tell you the number of times I have heard this statement: "I wish I would have met with you 20 years ago!" We can all take a proactive stance instead of a reactive approach. You can start by educating yourself on your federal benefits; which is what this book is all about.

When I decided to write this book, I set out to provide information that would help the federal employee take full advantage of their benefits, while at the same time understand the pitfalls associated with the federal benefit package. This book will help answer some of the most common questions like:

- When can I retire?
- How well will I retire?
- What happens to FEGLI when I retire?
- Should I keep the FEGLI options A B & C?
- What should my TSP contribution rate be?
- Should I buy back military time?
- Is my TSP-3 completed correctly?
- When should I elect social security?
- Should I roll my TSP to an IRA?
- ROTH or Traditional IRA?
- Can Medicaid effect my annuity payments?
- Do I have enough time to recover from TSP losses?

When it comes to your federal employee benefits, what you don't know "can" hurt you. Unwanted or not, you have formed a partnership with the federal government when you signed the forms to elect your benefit choices. As with any partnership, you must take an active role to get the most from that relationship. Standing on the sidelines and just letting things "happen" is a position that can cost you and your family.

View your benefits as a tool.

When you purchase a tool at the hardware store you don't bring it home, hang it on the wall, put it in storage and wait for it to perform the task you acquired it for. You make sure you understand how to use it so it accomplishes the task it is intended for, and to make sure you handle it properly so that it doesn't hurt you. My goal is to help you utilize the benefit tools that you have chosen in a manner that will help you achieve the goals, objectives and priorities for your retirement dreams. In addition, I will help you maximize your benefits while you are still working. So, grab your tools and let's get started! Our first project is just ahead.

PART ONE:

Maximizing Your Understanding

CHAPTER ONE:

The Grass is Always Greener...

Since we cannot get what we like, let us like what we can get.
—Proverb

In our work-a-day world we can lose sight of our blessings.

The negative around us can start to drag us down and, before you know it, the "woe is me" syndrome can set in. I'm no different. It's human nature. After a time, things start to come into focus and we realize we can make the best of what we have or move on to other opportunities.

The employment and benefit packages you have with the federal government are some of the best in the world. Of course, nothing is perfect and we have to take the good with bad. When it comes to your employee benefits, it is clear that there is a lot more positive than there is negative. The key to being content with your benefits is eliminating the confusion and taking advantage of all that it can be. Be thankful because with any career there will be ups and downs. This is something I hear on a regular basis: "I am happy to have stable government employment, a secure retirement and benefit package along with many other benefits." I will continue to remind you of that statement throughout the text!

Many employees become frustrated and confused about their benefits and, all too often, happiness turns into a sour attitude. Many times these frustrations are fueled by several factors, which include but are not limited to:

- Procedures that may seem outdated or antiquated.
- Knowing a more efficient way to solve a problem but government procedures and red tape get in the way.
- Creativity may be shunned for the sake of "procedure".
- Many times the government's answer to the problem is worse than the original problem you are trying to solve.
- Not being rewarded with a promotion you know you deserve because of seniority status.
- Having to take up the slack from a co-worker that simply does not do their job.

All in all, most employees I have polled will state that their government career is rewarding and provides the challenges they seek on a day-to-day basis. Although there are some disadvantages (what career doesn't have its share of disadvantages?), a career with the federal government is one of the best career paths anyone could take. Like anything in life, most of us tend to take things for granted. We get spoiled; especially in this great country, we are privileged. Just ask someone living in Haiti! There are other opportunities that seem, at times, better than the government employment option. If the time ever comes that you make the decision to leave your government career, take the time to review all of the facts before you make that final and sometime irreversible decision. Here are the facts:

The federal government has been in business for over 226 years. That is quite a heritage and testimony to the resiliency of our country!

The federal government has over 2.6 million employees on the payroll, so you can see why it is the country's largest employer. With annual revenues that exceed $3 trillion, it dwarfs many blue chip companies like General Motors or Wal-Mart. The opportunities offered by the federal government are vast and diverse. For example:

Attorney, FBI agent, Air Traffic Controller and, of course, the highest position -President of the United States.

Those facts alone should cause you to pause and reflect. Let us consider two other very important considerations for the government employee: job security and stability. In our current job environment, we consistently see employees of Fortune 500 companies like IBM, Sprint; and AT&T live with the daily concern of falling victim to the next massive layoffs. We now realize that businesses and companies, that were considered household names, are not immune to the threat of bankruptcy and closure. Remember Circuit City, Enron and MCI? As a federal employee, that is not a general concern. The U.S has approximately 285 million citizens. It is also the world's most powerful and stable nation. Those citizens will continue to require services such as: national security, interstate highways, consumer and environmental protection, an equitable justice system and many other government-provided services. The federal government continues to do business. History has shown that its annual growth has topped that of the U.S. economy combined.

Additionally we need to factor in job security: private employers for the most part do not have employment contracts in place. This allows private employers to fire employees at will. Private employees can be fired for any reason even if it seems unfair. As long as it does not violate federal or state laws against discrimination on the basis of race, gender or age, federal employees have a higher level of protection against unfair termination. They can only be let go for clearly defined reasons, which are primarily incompetence, dishonesty and fraud. Detailed grievance processes held before an un-biased board are available to federal employees to contest the premise of any employment action. I am sure that employment security is important to you, which makes the federal government employer a great choice.

The federal government has great compensation. The federal employer is required by law to pay workers at prevailing private sector wages. Title 5, section 5301, requires that federal salary and wage rates for white-collar employees must be competitive with the private-employer pay rates for similar careers within the same local area. This is accomplished by implementing two types of annual income adjustments. This is in the form of a general increase based upon changes within the Employment Cost Index (ECI) and locality wage adjustments. These are based upon general variations in wage levels within 32 geographical areas. It has been found that a portion of the country's larger private employers will at times pay a higher base wage than federal employers. Most are at a 10% or less difference. With that in mind, you have to assess the additional risk you would take by venturing into the private employer sector, since historically greater job security is found with the federal government. That slight difference in pay can become insignificant when you consider numerous perks and incentives provided to federal employees. These include locality adjustments, hardship differentials, cost-of-living allowances (for overseas duty), relocation bonuses, retention allowances, recruitment bonuses, incentive awards and student-loan repayment.

The additional compensation can really add up: it can account for 100% or more of base wages. As an example: a GS-13 grade federal employee working overseas might earn as much as $150,000 in some areas. Superior retirement benefits that federal employees take part in are a tremendous advantage over the private sector. A study conducted in 1998 by the Congressional Budget Office compared compensation levels of federal and non-federal employees. They found that a 35-year-old federal employee with 10 years of service earning $45,000 in annual salary would accrue over 51% more in retirement benefits for the year compared to his private-sector counterpart ($5,320 vs. $3,516). Take a look at this example: a 55-year-old with 20 years of service earning a $75,000 salary would accrue 31% more in retirement benefits ($14,435 vs. $10,998). The additional benefit to this retirement differential has even more impact based upon the days in which we live. The fact is that federal employees can transfer service credits among other federal government agencies. An Army officer with 6 years of military service can add his service time should he become a federal civilian employee. This type of credit is certainly not available in the private sector.

Additionally, a federal employee can secure a considerable amount of retirement credit at a young age. It is not out of the ordinary for a federal employee to retire at age 55 and receive as much as 80% of what they were earning during the high three year average. How about vacation time and holiday breaks? Federal employees receive an average of about 20% more paid vacation and holiday time than employees in private companies. Consider the fact that a new federal employee earns 4 hours of vacation time for each two-week pay period, or 13 vacation days per year. After three years of employment, vacation time accrues at the rate of six hours per pay period, or 20 days a year. A federal employee with 15 years of service earns five weeks of paid vacation time per year; which is in addition to the 10 paid holidays that all federal employees enjoy.

Competitive Health Insurance Benefits are probably the most complained about benefit in the private sector. We don't hear that much from the federal government employees. The fact is that federal employee health insurance benefits are designed to provide less coverage than the large private sector employers during the employee's working years. The coverage increases during retirement years. Did you know that a 35-year-old federal employee in 2008 with 10 years of service with a salary of $45,000 a year would receive $3,265 in health insurance benefits per year? That is 5% more than the $3,106 that the private sector provides for a 55-year-old with an annual salary of $75,000, the value of health insurance benefits would total $5,410 per year. That is 2.8% more than the $5,265 private-sector employee.

All federal employees accrue four hours of sick leave for each two weeks worked on the Disability and Sick Leave. Sick leave can also be used to care for family member needs. The Family Medical Leave Act provides for up to 12 weeks of time off (using accrued leave or leave without pay) per year for medical emergencies. Sick leave may be accumulated from year to year. This sick leave accumulation is intended to be your short term disability coverage. A federal employee's sick leave and disability benefits are far greater than those of private-sector employees to the tune of about 10% across the board. A wise man once told me that the grass may look greener on the other side, but when you get over there, that grass has to be mowed too!

CHAPTER TWO:

Taking a New Perspective on Learning

Tell me and I forget. Teach me and I remember. Involve me and I learn.
–Benjamin Franklin

The old saying goes: "You can't teach an old dog new tricks." I beg to differ. At the writing of this book I am turning 52. I have learned more about financial services and how to better advise my clients in the past five years than my 20 plus years in the industry combined. Why? Because I am *willing* to learn. I realized that I needed to become more educated on all of the details of IRA distribution.

I set out to gather as much information as possible. I attended webinars, seminars, ordered publications, scanned IRS forms and more. The results have been astounding. I learned about a little-known tax break called Net Unrealized Appreciation which has the potential to save my clients that hold company-owned stock in their 401k thousands of dollars in distribution taxes.

I am constantly seeking new information: it has become a habit and, ultimately, I have become a much more valuable resource to my clients. You can become a more valuable resource to yourself and your family if you are *willing* to learn.

This book is divided into two parts because, before you can take a grasp of new information, you need to rethink your thinking. It does no good to put on perfume before you take shower, if it just keeps the stink undercover even longer! The first part of this book will be the mental shower. This will remove the odor of misconceptions, misinformation and misunderstandings. You will then dry off and apply the perfume of knowledge which will enable you to get a "fresh" start so you understand and utilize your benefits more effectively. The following chapters contain the Earn While You Learn Philosophy. I believe that if you take the time to learn these principles, you will become a more productive employee and, in turn, have a more successful and enjoyable career. You will also be able to enjoy a more satisfying retirement by simply putting these concepts and facts into action. If you have had concerns or doubts about your federal career, this chapter should be an eye opener.

Now is the time to view things from a much more positive perspective. This will set the stage for a better managed career and life altogether. If your final decision is to leave federal service before you retire; the principles that you will learn from this book will help you get the most out of the time you do spend with the federal government. At the beginning of this book, we mentioned that you need to view your benefits as a tool. The success of that tool depends upon the person using that tool to its maximum potential. Now, let's look closer at this concept and determine how it can benefit you. You are probably acquainted with a couple of co-workers who view their finances from two diffcrent perspectives. They are financial opposites. They may even earn about the same and have very similar benefit packages. You may have observed this and asked yourself how two people can have the same tool at their disposal, yet end up with a much different outcome? I feel that, outside of tragic events and setbacks, lack of knowledge is the problem. How do you gain knowledge? By study and practice. Knowledge is power! I was inspired to write this book based upon my many years in the financial services profession. Daily contact with clients and prospective clients has brought me to many conclusions.

Lack of knowledge causes confusion. Confusion leads to frustration. Frustration leads to anger, which ultimately can lead to giving up. I have seen it over and over again, and the tragedy is that so much can be accomplished by simply gaining the knowledge needed through systematic study and a little self-discipline along the way.

One of my goals as an advisor is to dispel misconceptions and incorrect information. Once I accomplish that with a client, we can then start the journey with less chance of frustration. How do you feel about your knowledge of how your benefits work? Are there any misconceptions that you are struggling with? Here are some examples of common misconceptions. Test yourself on this True or False pop quiz:

1. The TSP is matched 15% if you are in management. (True or False)
2. If you want to cancel your FEGLI, you need to wait for an open enrollment. (True or False)
3. Open enrollment for FEGLI is once a year. (True or False)
4. If both you and your spouse are covered through the government health insurance and your spouse dies, the HR department will automatically reduce your premiums to reflect a single individual. (True or False)

This is a small sampling of misconceptions we hear from federal employees. So, how did you do on the pop quiz? The answers are:

1. False
2. False
3. False
4. False

Don't beat yourself up if you didn't fare so well. The federal employee benefit package is very unique and complex. Most financial advisors don't have a clue about your benefits, and rightfully so. The reason is because a financial advisor must seek out this information on their own, and for the most part, it is self-taught.

I have studied for and sat for many exams and continuing education programs over the years. None of them required me to know anything about federal employee benefits to maintain or acquire any of my licensing or certifications. The information in this book will help you bridge that gap. Take responsibility for your education and you will reduce the confusion about your benefits. This book is designed to cover all areas. Although that makes the book a bit lengthy; it will provide you with a resource for years to come. Misunderstandings and confusion are rampant across all sectors of the federal government in regards to your benefit package. We can't blame that on the government, your supervisor or OPM. What I want to make clear in this chapter, is that you must take responsibility for educating yourself and seeking out all resources that are available to you. The reality of it is that many federal employees view their benefits as a confusing bird's nest of terms and formulas that cannot be unraveled; they just stick their heads in the sand and convince themselves that everything will work out just fine with no effort on their part. Nothing could be further from the truth. Knowledge is power and you need to arm yourself with this power.

It is beneficial to know the history of the federal employee benefits system. This will give you a basis from which to work from as you study the current benefits package as it is now.

One thing is for sure, things are going to change. A major change took place in 1984 that totally revamped the retirement system. The original retirement system was called CSRS, or the Civil Service Retirement System. This system paid employees a guaranteed pension if they met certain requirements (age, years of service, etc.). Employees didn't have any additional responsibilities to ensure a pension. They still had to make choices concerning FEGLI and health insurance, but the pension was in place with no decisions made by the employee.

The success of the retirement pension was primarily based upon the employee's pay grade, years of service and spending habits. In 1984, the federal government introduced FERS, Federal Employee Retirement System. In this system, many of the benefits stayed the same. However, the pension annuity was completely overhauled. A typical 30-year career employee who was hired under FERS would receive about 20% less through his/her annuity. The 20% cut would need to be made up through the TSP investing and Social Security.

Before we move on, here is a suggestion, stay away from water cooler advice. You know the conversation. It happens during a break time or over lunch. You get into a short conversation with a well-meaning co-worker who seems to have all the answers. They are not shy to voice their opinion and their statements at times seem educated and spot on. As a veteran financial advisor, I can tell you that I have witnessed numerous negative situations concerning benefit under-standing that were caused by this "well meaning" co-worker. I am not an expert when it comes to diagnosing a problem with my vehicle. I leave that to the professionals; you know, those that are certified to disassemble a fuel injections system. If I gave advice on car repair, my friend would not be happy with the fact that they took my advice as the car sputters and spurts down the highway! For some reason there are those that think they are a financial expert because they listened to a few rants from the media produced "experts" on TV or radio. Many bad benefit and financial decisions are based upon what others are saying or doing. Most of what others are doing is based on what others said. Here is the problem with the "others". If you rely upon advice from the "others", what you will often find is an old-timer Civil Service employee giving their opinions about what fund alloca-tion is the best for TSP.

They may tell you how much life insurance coverage is best, etc. Every situation has its own unique set of circumstances. Taking gen-eral advice from "others" causes problems, it's as simple as that. There are no general situations. Everyone and every situation is unique, es-pecially when it comes to structuring the federal employee benefits package. There are numerous cultures, socioeconomic classes and per-sonality types that interact on a daily basis.

The only thing about federal employees that is the same is their benefits. The options on how to get the most out of those benefits is full of variables. Here are some examples where variables can become a problem when you take advice from "others".

- Creditable service date
- The number of years an employee will work
- The amount an employee commits to the TSP
- Spousal income
- The retirement of a spouse
- Investments outside the TSP
- Saving patterns and amounts
- Are there any inherited funds?
- Number of dependents
- Personal lifestyle
- Debt load
- Spending habits
- Health issues
- Spouse's health issues
- Spouse's insurance coverage
- Educational expenses
- Net assets
- Projected inflation rates at retirement
- Current and future tax bracket
- Current and future income requirements
- Investment risk tolerance
- Your personal timeline (more discussion on this later)
- Support of elderly parents
- The length of your career
- TSP performance
- And many more beyond this small sampling.

Do you have a water cooler advisor? Have your benefit decisions been influenced by the water cooler round table? We spoke about this earlier so we will continue with a typical scenario that I often see. Harry is our water cooler advisor.

But who is Harry? Is he CSRS or FERS? What license, certification or financial advisor education does Harry really have? As important as these decisions are, shouldn't these discussions be better left for a qualified professional?

Harry is well meaning, but whether he realizes it or not, his advice can be very confusing and, ultimately, a danger for the recipient of the advice. Unless Harry is a financial advisor or an expert employee in the personnel department, proceed with caution. Of course we can't blame Harry for all of our financial pitfalls. Let's just concentrate on your goals, objectives and priorities while we continue to seek out a better understanding of our federal employee benefits.

Let's examine the Three Phases of Life and Retirement plans:

1. Accumulation Phase: We accumulate the most assets in our earning years. This is when we are working full-time, building our nest egg, investing, putting money in our TSP and/or IRA accounts and trying our best to reduce or eliminate debt.

2. Preservation Phase: As retirement draws near, we focus less on accumulation and more on preservation; taking fewer risks with our nest egg and putting more in trusted bank CDs, fixed/fixed indexed annuities and other safe investments.

3. Distribution Phase: After accumulation and protection, we start thinking about distribution. How will we convert our pensions, TSP, IRAs and other assets into lifetime income? What phase are you in? What risks are you taking with your money? Are you seeking out distribution friendly investments? I will get into more detail on the subject of accumulation, protection and distribution in future chapters. But for now let's turn our attention to the foundation for all of this. Earn While You Learn Philosophies...

CHAPTER THREE:

Earn While You Learn Philosophies

Learning makes a man fit company for himself.
-Thomas Fuller

Developing a better understanding of your federal benefits works best if you take bite size chunks. Don't try to eat a chicken whole; start with the wing, then a thigh - one bite at a time. I know the digestive process is a little different than the learning process but you get the idea.

There are 6 philosophies that I use to build a solid foundation which will help you get the most out of the Federal Retirement System:

Philosophy #1- Retirement Is What You Make of It!

I have found that most federal employees put their time into a government service career assuming the retirement planning will take care of itself via the pension, Social Security, TSP contributions (if applicable) and a belief that the government will take care of them. Unfortunately, it is not until they reach retirement age that they discover four built-in traps that await federal employees who have not prepared a retirement plan.

1. They forget that the IRS has a vested interest in their distributions which can cause surprising tax liabilities.

2. The FEGLI life insurance options they have chosen become unaffordable which leaves the employee under-insured at the time of need.
3. The TSP allocations have left the employee with market and or inflation risk.
4. The one I see the most is the fear of outliving their money.

We touched on Earn While You Learn Philosophy #1 earlier. Let's go into more detail on this very important segment.

I find that the blame game can rear its ugly head when a person suddenly realizes that their retirement plan is not what they thought or assumed it would be. In most cases, it is those individuals that take responsibility for their own actions and seize every opportunity possible to improve themselves and take the challenges that life brings. It is our own human nature that will tend to take the easy way out and just hope the obstacles and challenges will go away. Sometimes it will work but, unfortunately, we have to address the problems and challenges head on.

You can try to side step your responsibilities, but you can't side step the consequences of shirking your responsibilities. This first philosophy builds a foundation for everything else. Taking responsibility for your decisions will set the stage for success. Success is where you find it. People from all walks of life and various circumstances, federal employees or otherwise, have had more or less obstacles and have found options that worked for them. Keep a positive attitude and work with what you have and build on it one step at a time. Eliminate the excuses. Are you too busy? Is your budget tight? Do you have too much debt? There are always going to be things that will stand in your way. Resolve to stand firm in the face of these distractions so that you can develop a system of personal accountability. We will help you overcome the obstacles and setbacks. Yes, we are here to help you on this journey! Federal employees who take advantage of a positive mindset and make the decision to get their financial lives in order are suddenly more confident. And definitely more educated to determine what is needed to consistently stay on track. I have heard from so many of my clients about a sense of accomplishment and security they feel by grasping Philosophy # 1. They had the courage to take the first step.

Philosophy #2: Your Financial World.

Throughout my travels and federal benefit planning workshops, I am often asked about TSP rollover options and which is the best way to go. Federal employees want to know more about the FEGLI options, and if their selection was a good one, etc. My objective is to always provide solid information and provide the best possible answers. Remember our quote from Mr. Benjamin Franklin at the beginning of chapter two: "Tell me and I forget. Teach me and I remember. Involve me and I learn." Remember Harry earlier in the book? I strive not to be "Harry". Many times I am asked questions that don't have a definitive answer. That answer usually depends upon a number of factors that relate to the specifics of that employee's personal circumstances and includes many possible variables mentioned earlier. There is no one-size-fits-all system when it comes to the complexity of life changing questions. A good plan for one employee may not be for another, and vice versa. This is why we put so much emphasis on the first philosophy.

This chapter will show you where to direct your focus and energy. My goal is to give you the vision you need to succeed. Focus on managing your mind, than you can manage your benefits. This is why I want to make sure before answering a question that the employee is not skipping this very important step. Your finances and most aspects of your life are controlled more by what is going on between your ears than anything else. Two financial concepts for you to think about are the general financial world and your financial world. We have very little, if any, control over the general financial world (bailouts, income tax rates, inflation, rates of return); but you do have control over *your* financial world. There are many people getting along just fine financially in what is considered a down economic environment and there are those who do poorly in the best of economic times. The easy way out is to blame the "economy". And why wouldn't we? After all, we are constantly bombarded with negative scare tactic media. It is easy to succumb to the constant negative rhetoric. In good times or in bad; in busts or in booms, as a country we have proven our resiliency.

Put the economy in terms of your thoughts and attitudes that make it what it is. The status of a current economy does not determine a successful career or retirement, but rather a philosophy. If you watch 10 minutes of the world news you can come to the conclusion that the world is in a bad state of affairs.

Since you have control over what you watch and listen to, you can also take control of how you perceive and act on those things. The economic times we are currently living in is a time that presents tremendous opportunity for many people, but especially for those who make the most of what is available to them. Our history has shown that triumph has come out of hard times and adversity. These triumphs and historical events should give you a feeling of hope about the future. The news media will try to convince you that we are in the second Great Depression. After that 10-year period of time in our history, many thought our world as we knew it was over. But consider the tremendous advancements that have taken place in our world since that terrible time. Walk through a mall or an electronics store, or drive a late model car. Consider the technology we have at our finger tips—laptops, software, GPS, the world wide web, email, cell phones, space shuttles, digital cameras, iPods, text messaging, wireless headsets, Bluetooth, Blackberry, iPhones, microwaves, HDTV, DirecTV, YouTube and a car that can parallel park itself.

Facebook and Twitter were not even words during the Great Depression. This is the kind of advancement that rebounds from economic hardship. The fact is the Great Depression produced a number of successful landmarks that are still with us today. I am sure you are familiar with companies like Readers Digest, Time magazine,

The New Yorker, Walt Disney and Mickey Mouse, the Boeing 247 and the Douglas DCs, Pitney Bowes, Betty Crocker, the Band Aid, Caterpillar Tractor, A&W Root Beer, the bagel, Gerber, Mrs. Stover's, Pan American, Roto-Rooter, State Farm, Kleenex, Avon, Blue Cross, Clairol, Revlon, Hostess, Wonder Bread, Dolly Madison, White Castle, Hewlett-Packard, Kellogg's, Post, Proctor & Gamble and Chevrolet. Communication grew rapidly through advancements in radio and print, the FDIC and SEC were formed. This is just a few of the many good things that came out of the Great Depression.

You can see that those who embrace change as opportunity and realize progress can come out of hard times victorious. So keep it all in perspective, in most cases it is a state of mind. Don't get me wrong, I have seen bad times and have thought of giving up. We will always have opportunity mixed with adversity and adversity mixed with opportunity. How true that statement is! So, start looking for the positives instead of worrying about the negative.

Stay away from envy and complaining; crunch the numbers, and make some changes. Get motivated to make a difference in yours and your family's lives. Earl Nightingale once said, "If the grass is greener on the other side, it's probably getting better care." A path to success in your career and retirement is not all about your benefits package, FEGLI selections, bank accounts or your TSP management, but it can be about your attitude.

Philosophy #3: Establish Your Long-Term Game Plan for Long-Term Success.

When I have the opportunity to consult with a young start-up employee, presenting a long term financial plan is usually difficult for them to comprehend. When I reflect on my life and planning when I was in my early 20's, I have to say that I was very short sighted. Ten years seemed like forever and 20 or more seemed like an eternity.

Now I look back on that time and it seems like it was yesterday. My how time flies!

Most 20 year olds are focused on establishing themselves in their career and raising a family. Retirement seems like a foreign land that will be ready when they get there. When I start to develop their plan that may project 30 or 40 years into the future, it becomes clear to most of them that small decisions can greatly impact their financial future. They soon realize that something as simple as a ROTH IRA program with a $50 per pay period contribution will grow to an amount that seems inconceivable. Soon they learn about the time value of money. Your bank loan officer and the IRS are very familiar with the time value of money—are you? Many times I will get a call a few months after the initial consultation and the new client will increase their contribution. I have heard many times: "You know, I thought that $50 per pay period was going to be a stretch, but I don't even miss it. Let's go ahead and increase it."

I love it when a plan comes together! Since I set this client up with a ROTH program that has no stock market risk and layers of guarantees and protection, they know it will never lose value. This client will benefit from the miracle of compound interest, day by day, week by week, and year by year. The money is working for the client. Rate of return never sleeps! Based upon incremental increases in contribution over time; this client will have a substantial nest egg for retirement. Happy is the man that finds wisdom and gains understanding! Wisdom is more valuable than gold. Benjamin Franklin, whom we quoted earlier, also said that an investment in knowledge always pays great dividends. Many people have the misconception that wisdom is for the super intellectual or the person with a long list of degrees or letters behind their name. But the fact is, wisdom is little more than the experiences we learn from putting the positives to work in our own lives, and to those whom we can extend a helping hand. Wisdom should be recognized as a means to living a full, blessed life that can be passed on to others so they can be blessed as well. This is how I feel about my practice.

I make my living educating people on all of the complexities of the financial world. I simplify it so that it is not intimidating and they can see and understand why it will help them. Wisdom is when you know you should be setting aside funds for the future, taking advantage of the time value of money. Wisdom is recognizing the need to have a better understanding of your benefits and implementing change when needed and making educated decisions

The wise are not always seen as the popular group. They may opt out of the happy hour and spend that time attending a TSP workshop, meeting with an advisor, or doing an annual review to make sure they stay on track. Are you establishing a long term game plan?

Philosophy #4: Knowledge Learned is Money Earned.

Have you ever committed to some type of self-improvement? A new exercise program is usually the most common. Day one gets here and you are trying to get yourself in the right frame of mind to overcome procrastination and to get the ball rolling. The exercise machines feel a bit awkward and you may feel somewhat out of place. But after a few days things start to click. You're not as sore and, in fact, you start to feel a bit more comfortable.

It's like wearing a new pair of shoes. There is a break-in period. Committing to a solid financial plan is no different. A little awkward and intimidating at first, but then you start to see progress. All this financial terminology starts to make sense.

When you speak with your advisor, the conversations take on a whole new meaning and you wonder why you ever waited this long to commit. So, you start charting your progress by tracking the performance of your investments; looking for ways to trim the budget so you can put more money in your plan.

Could you imagine a sports team that never kept score or never checked the stop watch? How would they know if they were winning or losing? And would they even care about the outcome of the game? The numbers are how we keep track of the score. Figures tell us how we must face the facts.

There are two statements I like to use when it comes to understanding and utilizing your federal benefits:

1. If you don't measure, you don't improve.
2. If you don't commit now you will fall behind.

Where am I now? Where do I want to be? What steps do I need to take to improve? How much time am I willing to commit? These are questions that can guide you as you move forward in the process of maximizing your benefits. One of the hardest things to do when getting started is forcing yourself to take a self-evaluation, or what I like to call a financial check-up. A simple self-examination will give you a reality check on your personal finances. Although this can be uncomfortable at first, you will find that it pays great dividends down the road. Let's face it, most of us would rather avoid looking in the mirror. Gaining a better understanding of your benefits and other financial issues will not require that you make a career out of it. There is no required exam at the end of this book, no continuing educational requirements or regulatory compliance you must follow. This is not rocket science. I have seen where a minor adjustment can make a huge difference and produce great results.

Some of you know that I am an avid bass angler. You may be thinking, yeah, well what does that have to do with all this financial stuff? The answer is, absolutely nothing. But since I am the author of this book I can use whatever analogies I want. Just kidding! You know I have found that even the slightest change in the way you present a bait, maybe change the color, or the speed of retrieve (I know all you hardcore anglers are getting this) can mean the difference between catching one or two and filling out a limit. Little things can and do matter. Most financial situations I am presented with require minor changes in order to improve the game plan.

Many will ignore the need for change altogether because they see it as too intimidating or bottom line; it is just too much trouble. Procrastination is the biggest killer of progress and reaching the goals that have been set. Setting up an organized positive habit is paramount to this process.

I like to see my clients develop an "organized positive habit". It's putting together a goal-oriented, step-by-step plan on paper and developing a habit of following that plan. And, by the way, in case you did not know, it takes 21 days to develop a new habit—good or bad. Will that plan need to be tweaked and changed along the way? Of course, and that is what will keep you enthused! Following through on these promises we make to ourselves is not easy, we know that. But if you put it down on paper and stay organized, your chances for success will increase dramatically.

You may be asking yourself, put what down on paper? I have no idea where to start. I can help you with that. We have the resources available to put you on track. All you have to do is call.

Philosophy # 4: This is All About Putting Some Pep in Your Step.

This philosophy is about putting your goals, objectives and priorities into action. You can put your own organized positive habit in place and strive to reach your goals. It starts with the first step. Don't use the "it's too late" excuse. No matter where you currently stand concerning your benefits and finances, it can always be improved no matter your age. Do not get discouraged by how much debt you may have or how little retirement savings you have amassed. Develop the habit and seek the results. Remain positive even if the account is zero. Start now with whatever you have. Where would you be today if you had started your savings habit three years ago? Forget about the past and think about where you will be three years from now if you commit to getting started today!

Philosophy #5: Don't Just Say It Or Think It. DO IT!

My experience has been that most of us are all in or all out. Which makes good sense. Most don't like lukewarm coffee, they like it hot. Same goes for a soft drink. It needs to be icy cold or we forget about having one.

Some become obsessed with saving and others don't give it a second thought. Effectively utilizing your employee benefits is an exercise in understanding the details and giving oneself an occasional tune-up, so to speak. You don't wash your car every day, but you don't wait until there is an inch of dirt collected before you wash it. Spend some extra time in the beginning working on the details and then it's easy to keep a refresher going from time to time. Procrastination is something we all battle, some more than others. I have found that if you take the time to write down the tasks you need to accomplish and check them off as you go, it will go a long way in nipping the old procrastination habit in the bud. How do you eat an elephant? One bite at a time! Same goes with killing procrastination. I think most folks get frustrated when they are saddled with a laundry list of must do's and keep putting them off until they get to the point of no return.

It reminds me of case I was working on a couple of years ago. This employee was trying to make a decision on their TSP rollover. I was able to structure a lifetime income benefit through an annuity that included an upfront bonus of 5% and a guaranteed roll-up percentage of 8%. I understand that these decisions are difficult ones, but this employee missed out on the 8% roll-up because the carrier reduced the rate to 7%. I made the employee aware of the need to do their research in a timely manner because these rates can change. They procrastinated on the research and lost out on additional future income. Have you ever heard the old saying "paralysis by analysis"? Of course we need to conduct our due diligence when making such important decisions, but at the same time don't miss out on a great opportunity by putting off what needs to be done in order to capitalize on such opportunities. When you start this journey, resolve to not let the procrastination bug get the best of you. Commit to your goals and accept the fact that there will bumps in the road along the way. You can DO IT!

Philosophy #6: Establish Your Goals and Stay on Track.

I have heard it said that the only thing for certain in this life is death and taxes. That is debatable because one part was left out. Change. I can guarantee you one thing for sure, and that is—things are going to change. Now, that probably doesn't make you feel any better but the fact is, change is a constant. How we deal with change is the real issue.

Do you fear change, or see it as an opportunity to grow, experience new things and capitalize on the moment? As we start each day, we prepare for those possible changes that may come our way. The employee meeting where new announcements are made that could change the way you are to conduct your business. The evening news telling us about the changes proposed concerning a city ordinance. Market news giving us an update on the change in the DJIA and S&P 500 values. The list goes on and on. A bit mind boggling if you think about it. If you deny change, which is in operation 24/7, you will not be prepared to deal with change when it inevitably occurs.

Face change with open arms and embrace it. After all, if you do not embrace change, it will embrace you. No doubt you have experienced change with your benefits. Ever had any of your TSP funds allocated in the C, S or I fund? Then you know about change for sure! Adapting to change is a habit well learned. To stay on top of your benefits you will need to keep pace with these changes. Rates, insurance premiums and total benefits can change. We can benefit from change only if we stay away from the fear factor. Some of the best experiences in my life have come as a result of major changes that took place. In most cases I had no control over the circumstances. I was forced to adapt. Painful at times? Yes, but rewarding in most. Think of a change you experienced that at first seemed devastating, then as you adapted to the change how differently you viewed it as time passed. Look for the opportunity in change, don't fear it! Let me relate a real world scenario that a federal employee can relate to. When I conduct a benefits review for an employee, one of the benefits that I spend a lot of time with is the review of FEGLI optional selections. When the employee has option B, I have found that the vast majority are not aware of the negative changes that are going to take place as they age. The premium will start to double in cost every five years at age 55 and beyond. This is a change you need to be aware of. Most are not aware of the 75% reduction of the basic life is at age 65 or retirement whichever is later. Recognizing these changes before they cost you will take a proactive stance on your part. Taking the time to conduct regular reviews will keep you on track with these changes.

PART TWO:

Optimizing Your Benefits

CHAPTER FOUR:

Understanding FEGLI

Now, let's get into a more detailed discussion concerning your Federal Employees Group Life Insurance, also known as FEGLI. Life insurance is an important component of your benefits package. I have found that this is the most misunderstood part of the benefits program. You need to have a thorough understanding of this very important coverage. All career employees can take part in the FEGLI coverage. Interpretation of the FEGLI code is the best starting point. This is how you determine what coverage you have chosen. Keep in mind that postal employees are the only federal employees that receive Basic Life coverage at no cost.

The FEGLI code begins with the letters IN followed by a number, a letter (or number 9) and then a number. The number following the IN indicates your age group, and the corresponding rates for each insurance:

1 = under 35	2 = 35-39	3 = 40-44
4 = 45-49	5 = 50-54	6 = 55-59
7 = 60-64	8 = 65-69	9 = 70 and over

The next letter, or number 9, indicates which options you have elected.

A – Ineligible

B - No Benefits

C - BL

D - BL, A

E - BL, C

F - BL, A, C

G - BL, Bx1

H - BL, A, Bx1

I - BL, C, Bx1

J - BL, A, C, Bx1

K - BL, Bx2

L - BL, A, Bx2

M - BL, C, Bx2

N - BL, A, C, Bx2

O - BL, Bx3

P - BL, A, Bx3

Q - BL, C, Bx3

R - BL, A, C, Bx3

S - BL, Bx4

T - BL, A, Bx4

U - BL, C, Bx4

V - BL, A, C, Bx4

W - BL, Bx5

X - BL, A, Bx5

Y - BL, C, Bx5

Z - BL, A, C, Bx5B

L = Basic Life

A = Option A

B = Option B

C = Option C

The final number, 0, 1, 2, 3, 4 or 5, shows the number of units selected with Option C, if any. If you did not elect Option C coverage, this will be a zero. NOTE: Since postal workers receive Basic Life coverage at no charge, their pay stub may not have an IN code if they did not elect any additional optional coverage. The Basic Life coverage will appear on their annual Statement of Benefits, though it does not appear on the pay stub.

Basic Life Insurance Coverage

As we mentioned, postal workers get this coverage at no charge. All other branches pay $0.15 per $1,000 of coverage. Basic Coverage is calculated using your Base Pay. You can calculate your Basic Coverage by taking your Base Pay - round it up to the next thousand, add $2,000 and that equals Total Basic Coverage. Consider this simple example. Bob has a base pay of $45,300. His Basic Coverage would be: $45,300 (Base Pay) $46,000 (Rounded Up) + $2,000 equaling $48,000 which is his Total Basic Coverage. As you get pay raises and COLAs, your Basic Coverage will also increase. You use the exact same calculation, with your new base pay after each raise. Your Final Expense Benefit and your Basic Life Insurance includes a little-known and seldom-claimed final expense benefit. If you retire prior to age 65, your Basic Life Insurance will remain in effect until age 65. For the next 38 months, it will reduce by 2% each month until the benefit reaches 25% of the original amount. Example: If Bob earns $52,000 at retirement, his Basic Insurance coverage is $54,000 until age 65. Over the next 3 years and 2 months, his coverage will reduce each month until it reaches $13,500 (25%). Most federal employees are not aware of the fact that this coverage stays in effect for life. Because most employees and their beneficiaries are unaware of this final expense benefit, it goes unclaimed in many cases. To take advantage of this added benefit, inform your Executor and your beneficiaries of this information. Put a note with your will, final papers and insurance documents. Beneficiaries should call the Retirement Information Office at 1-888-767-6738 for assistance.

Extra Benefit - Your Basic Coverage has an additional feature called the Extra Benefit. The Extra Benefit is basically a Bonus on your Basic

Coverage for being under the age of 45. Employees who are under the age of 45 will get a multiple of their Basic Coverage depending on their age. The ages and the applicable multiples are listed below:

<35= 2.0	36= 1.9	37= 1.8
38= 1.7	39= 1.6	40= 1.5
41= 1.4	42= 1.3	43= 1.2
44= 1.1	45= 0.0	

Let's look at an example to show you how the Extra Benefit would work. Let's take Bob again who has a Basic Coverage of $48,000 from our previous example. Let's also assume Bob is 39 years old, which qualifies him for the Extra Benefit. Bob's Extra Benefit would be calculated by taking his Basic Pay and multiplying that amount by the Extra Benefit Factor of 1.6 from our previous chart: Basic Life Coverage: $48,000 Extra Benefit Factor: x 1.6 Total Basic & Extra Benefit: $76,800. It's important to understand that when Bob turns 40, his Extra Benefit will be reduced to 1.5 and continue to reduce as he gets older until he turns 45 and will have no Extra Benefit. The current insurance company who has the life insurance contract through the government is willing to give you this additional Extra Benefit at no cost because you are younger and less likely to pass away. For all federal employees, the Cost of Basic Coverage is $0.15 per thousand dollars of coverage. An employee with $50,000 of Basic Coverage would pay $7.50 a pay period for that insurance. Remember, Extra Benefit insurance is at no additional cost.

Living Benefits Act

The next area of your FEGLI coverage is the Living Benefits Act. Very few federal employees are aware of this part of their benefits, but it is a critical subject and worth covering. The Living Benefits Act was passed in 1995. It was intended to benefit employees diagnosed with terminal illnesses. Under the Living Benefits Act, if an employee is diagnosed with a terminal illness and has 9 months or fewer to live, the employee can access his or her full Basic Coverage plus any applicable Extra Benefit at the time of diagnosis. This coverage allows ill employees to receive their benefits while they are living. This valuable coverage can allow employees to spend their final days with family and spare their loved ones the financial concerns that often accompany a terminal illness. Unfortunately, this coverage is very rarely used because most employees are unaware of this option. Please make your loved ones aware of this valuable coverage and if you have co-workers who could use this coverage, bring it to their attention.

Optional Insurance

Options A, B and C each add a different benefit to the FEGLI package. Employees can choose to add these when they are hired. These benefits may be reduced or cancelled at any time, but can only be added or increased during an open season which OPM occasionally offers, or following a qualifying event such as marriage, divorce or birth of a child.

OPTION A: This coverage is something you elected to pay for when you were hired. Option A is a very straight forward coverage under your FEGLI. It provides a $10,000 death benefit to beneficiaries in the event of the employee's death. Like most FEGLI insurance, the price does increase every 5 years, but because the coverage is so small, the cost is usually not an issue. Some employees refer to this coverage as a very affordable burial policy.

OPTION B: This life insurance option is very popular among federal employees. This option allows employees to take anywhere from 1 all the way up to 5 times their base pay in additional life insurance if they choose to pay for it. In most cases, this decision is made when the employee is hired. A simple example would be if Bob has a $50,000 base salary and he took 5x Option B he would have an additional $250,000 of life insurance coverage. The cost of this coverage is based upon your age. The government devised the plan and pricing.

A list of prices per thousand dollars of insurance coverage (rates effective as of January 1, 2012) is listed below. As you can see the cost rises dramatically at age 50 and beyond.

Federal Employees' Group Life Insurance (FEGLI) Program Rates:

Option B Premium per $1,000 of Insurance Age Band	Biweekly	Monthly
Under 35	$0.02	$0.043
35–39	$0.03	$0.065
40–44	$0.05	$0.108
45–49	$0.08	$0.173
50–54	$0.13	$0.282
55–59	$0.23	$0.498
60–64	$0.52	$1.127
65-69	$0.62	$1.343
70-74	$1.14	$2.470
75-79	$1.80	$3.900
80 and over	$2.40	$5.200

As you can see from the chart, rates increase as you age. They don't increase very quickly until age 50, and then things get very costly, very fast. The reason they increase is because the employee did not have to take a physical to get this additional coverage. The only thing the insurance company knows about you is your age, so that is the basis they use to increase coverage. As you get older, you are more likely to pass away so they charge you more.

*Special Note: You want to look for life insurance in the private sector, which could be more cost effective and offer more benefits. Almost any insurance plan you find in the private sector will provide a level death benefit and level premiums as well. For example, using rates available in the private sector today, a healthy 40-year-old male will pay $250 in annual premiums for $250,000 of coverage and that price will be locked in for 20 years. Under FEGLI rates, to get that same $250,000, a 40-year-old employee will pay $390 in annual premiums for 5 years, $585 each year for the next 5 years, $910 per year between the ages of 50 and 54, and a whopping $1,820 each year from 55 to 59 years of age. At age 60, under the current FEGLI rates, that amount will more than double. Currently, in the private market, a healthy 50-year-old male can lock in rates for 20 years on $250,000 for annual premiums of around $625. As a general rule, if you are healthy, you are better off getting your life insurance with a private company and protecting yourself from the increases the federal program allows. If you are unable to obtain approval from a private company, keeping the federal life insurance until you cannot afford the price may be your best option.

Very few people in the federal government understand the details of their life insurance program. The cost of not understanding how the program works can cost the employee thousands of dollars in premiums they wouldn't have paid if they had known what you just learned. If you just figured out that you may be paying too much for your federal insurance, check and see what a private company could do for you in terms of a replacement policy. Those of you who would like our assistance can contact a Benefit Specialist by calling our corporate office at 417-429-0331. Our comparison quote allows us to compare several different companies to ensure we find the best price possible.

OPTION C: This is your Family Coverage provision, and is an optional coverage you elect to pay when hired on with the government. Family Coverage is life insurance on your family where you will be the beneficiary should one of your family members pass away. Family Coverage is offered in units. An employee can take 1-5 units of Family Coverage. Each unit represents $5,000 on your spouse and $2,500 on each dependent child. Dependent children are defined as unmarried children under the age of 22, and unmarried foster and adopted children living with you in a parent-child relationship under the age of 22. Let's look at an example of an employee who took 5 units of Family Coverage. With 5 units, the spouse will be covered for $25,000 and each dependent child will be covered for $12,500. It is important to note that there is no limit to the number of dependent children covered under your Family Coverage. Another important aspect of Option C is you cannot drop part of the coverage. For example, if your dependent children leave, you cannot drop the coverage on your children and keep the coverage on your spouse. When it comes to Family Coverage, you either have it or you don't.

CHAPTER FIVE:

Thrift Savings Plan (TSP)

The Thrift Savings Plan (TSP) was implemented as part of the Federal Retirement benefits package and serves as a vehicle to accumulate retirement funds. Technically it is NOT a 401k because it falls under the direction and control of Congress. For the purpose of understanding how it works, it shares most of the pluses and minuses of all other 401k plans. On the plus side, in 1984 when the FERS program was started, Congress established 5% matching funds for FERS employees as an incentive to encourage retirement savings. This is one of the best programs in the country, and provides FREE MONEY to FERS employees for their retirement. The government will contribute 1% of a FERS employee's salary to their TSP fund whether they choose to contribute or not. (This is separate from the FERS retirement fund, and is vested after 3 years.) They will also match the first 3% of an employee's contributions dollar for dollar, and 50 cents for every dollar of the next 2% the employee puts in, making a total of 5% government funds to match the first 5% of an employee's contribution. These are funds you cannot make up later, so it is beneficial to maintain a 5% contribution to the TSP from day one of eligibility. A FERS employee can build a substantial nest egg by sticking to this savings pattern, and allow the government to provide them a 100% return on this money.

The TSP also has a lot of the same pitfalls of the 401k. First, it was originally designed as a tax shelter, but has never been as effective as intended. In a 401k, taxes are deferred on contributions while an employee is working and are assessed as income when the funds are withdrawn during retirement. The theory was that this would be at a lower tax rate, thereby creating a tax shelter on both the contributions and the earnings. The tax savings have been minimal from the beginning. The cost of living has steadily increased, as has the standard of living. Inflation doesn't stop at retirement. While pensions and Social Security checks are significantly less than the employee's paycheck while they were working, adding a spouse's retirement income and taking withdrawals from savings will frequently result in an end-of-the-year tax bracket that is similar to pre-retirement rates. And those rates continue to climb. In fact, most 401k funds that are withdrawn in retirement are assessed at an equal or higher tax rate than they would have been when they were deposited. Many retirees experience no tax savings through 401k income, and will see as much as one-third of their funds lost to taxes.

Second, until an employee reaches the age of 59 1/2, 401k funds are inaccessible without penalty or interest. The IRS is your silent partner who will demand their part during distributions. In fact, they will demand their portion when you turn 70 years old. This is known as Required Minimum Distribution. Because taxes have not been paid, the IRS regulates those funds very carefully and has a vested interest in the account. If you withdraw funds prior to age 59 1/2, you must pay a 10% penalty plus count the withdrawal as income for the year, and pay taxes accordingly. The exception to this rule is if you leave service at age 55 or older; you can take distribution without incurring the 10% premature distribution penalty. You will still be required to report this as income in the year you take the distribution. This is unique to the TSP program. To my knowledge there are no other qualified plans that provide this special IRS provision. Another option is to borrow the money (from yourself) and repay yourself with interest.

One of the unique features of the TSP plan set up by Congress for federal employees is that if you retire from federal service prior to age 59 1/2 and have not paid a penalty for a previous withdrawal, you may roll your TSP funds into a qualified plan without penalty. Contact Federal Employee Benefit Advisors prior to starting your separation to make sure you understand your options. An additional problem with the TSP is that the investment options it offers are very low return or very high risk. The past few years point out the dangers of tying retirement funds to the market. If you are a federal employee, you're well aware of the fact that the vast majority of your co-workers lost money in their TSP after October 2007. Many lost more money in 2008 than they earned in wages during the same period. Those who didn't lose were primarily in the G fund and gained around 3%. Remember, one-third of that will be taken out in taxes, so the resulting gain will be slightly less than the cost of living increase over the same period. In other words, even at its best; in a down market, the TSP produced a zero or negative return on investment.

The TSP has a tax liability. Taxes will have to be paid on all contributions and interest. In the event of the premature death of the employee, those taxes can be at the highest assessed rate. The 401k has proven to be a windfall for the government to collect taxes when an employee dies leaving money in the account. In this case, the entire balance is distributed to the beneficiaries and charged as income for the year. This means that a surviving spouse may now be pushed into the maximum tax bracket that year. Finally, many employees are depending on their TSP as their only supplement to Social Security and their pension. Virtually everyone who does this will be required to take a pay cut in retirement. Even with the matching funds, 5% savings is not enough to build a retirement income equal to their previous paycheck, especially if those investments rise and fall with the market. While most people know they should be saving more, very few do; and unmatched funds in the TSP are subject to the disappointments of the low-return / high-risk options.

Have you ever wondered how much you should put away for retirement? The answer will vary according to individual needs in retirement. Generally, if we start before age 30 and invest 10% of every dollar we make until age 65, we will retire at an equal or better income than we are accustomed to. If we wait until after age 30 to start saving, we will need to put away 12-15% to reach that same goal. And if you are over 40, you may need to put away 15% or more to build a comfortable retirement income.

A Real World Example

I am providing the following example courtesy of a federal employee who shared his game plan with us.

Every employee has unique circumstances, and of course yours may be different. This employee's experience explains how he made the most of his TSP investments. He stayed away from the C, S, I and Lifecycle funds to eliminate any possibility of losing any of those hard earned dollars. He was able to get a predictable and positive return on the investment. This FERS employee always contributed 5% to the Thrift Savings Plan. Since the government matches his 5% with an additional 5%, he knows he has an immediate 100% return on investment. He kept his funds allocated to the G fund, where it has no risk of loss. Although it's not all that exciting he knows that he has already doubled his money. He can sleep well knowing that he will not experience any losses. Based upon his salary, 5% is just a little over $100 each pay period, or about $2,700 per year. His contribution plus the matching funds from the government and the interest on the entire balance helped his TSP account grow by almost $6,000 last year while many of his co-workers lost thousands. His plan is to retire within 13 years. Based upon his contribution rate the total will be in the $35,000 range. Taking into consideration the matching funds and moderate but consistent interest rate, his TSP will grow by another $100,000. With other investments, he will have enough for retirement.

This example shows us that by saving $5,000 per year at 2-5% interest will grow to an estimate of $150,000 in a 20-year career. That can add a considerable amount of monthly income during retirement, and help fill the income gap many employees face when they retire. I have seen many employees with the same benefit plan as their co-workers and yet one employee was forced to seek employment in retirement, yet another who had more income in retirement than when they were employed by the government. There are guaranteed interest and tax-free funds available that most federal employees are unaware of. For a federal employee making $52,000 year, 10% means saving $200 each paycheck for retirement. If you are like most employees I visit with, you are over 30 and have not started putting away the amount necessary to provide a secure retirement. You may be like the thousands of people starting over because of life's little roadblocks that seem to get in the way at the worst possible time. You know the list: bankruptcy, divorce, refinance, kids, failed business ventures, health issues, etc... The good news is there is hope! The difficult part is that you need to become more aggressive and educated about your retirement investments. Take some time to review your budget and determine where you can make some cuts. You need to find $100, $200 or even $300 per paycheck over and above the 5% matching contribution to the TSP, and invest it regularly and wisely.

CHAPTER SIX:

All About Your Health Benefits

Many federal employees choose their health plan by throwing a dart at the wall and hope that it lands on the right spot. This is not the approach I would recommend. During open season, federal employees have the opportunity to review their health benefit options. Although benefits change within the plans and premiums continue to increase annually; many federal employees leave their health insurance choices to chance and never look at a plan other than the one they have. The reasons can vary. Maybe they are content with the current plan and they simply do not want to expend the energy or time looking at other choices. This chapter is focused on the process of comparing health plans and breaking them down so you can compare and understand the variety of plan choices.

The following are standard rules that apply to all plans:

- During open season, which is usually the second Monday in November through the second Monday in December, federal employees and retirees may enroll in, change or cancel their existing health plan. They can also choose to enroll in, change or cancel their dental and vision coverage. And in order to participate in the flexible savings account for the following year, employees must state how much they want to contribute for the year.

- All federal health plans are required to have a no pre-existing condition clause. This allows federal employees to move from one plan to another during open season each year without being concerned about any existing health conditions. Each plan must take your enrollment no matter what your health condition. This continues even when you are retired.
- Each plan also is required to have a maximum out-of-pocket limit for the year. If you reach that limit, you will not be required to pay any further expenses, co-pays and deductibles due to this limit. The amount of the out-of-pocket limit varies from plan to plan, so you will want to be sure you understand the maximum amount you would have to pay out of your own pocket for the plans you are considering.

Here are some standard definitions you may want to become familiar with:

FEHB – Federal Employee Health Benefits

FEDVIP – Federal Employee Dental and Vision Insurance Plan

PCP – Primary Care Physician

FSA – Flexible Savings Account

HSA – Health Saving Account

HMO – Health Maintenance Organization

PPO – Preferred Provider Organization

FFS – Fee-For-Service Plan

HDHP – High Deductible Health Plan

IOU – What you see if you don't have good insurance

Traditional Types of Health Plans

HMO- Health Maintenance Organization. This is coverage where you choose a primary care physician from a list of member physicians to provide your general health care. Any visits to a specialist must be referred by your Primary Care Physician (PCP). There is typically no coverage for out-of-network care with the exception of emergency care. You are not required to pay a deductible, but there are often co-pays associated with office visits and prescriptions.

PPO – Preferred Provider Organization. This is a group of contracted providers who you can select from. You do not have to name one particular provider to be your primary care physician and can visit any doctor as long as they are on the preferred provider list. These plans vary by state with many different options available around the country. You are not required to stay within the network, but the insurer will pay more if you do. Typically, your insurance company might pay 80% and you would pay 20% if you went to someone on the preferred provider list. If you went out-of-network, the insurer might only pay 70% and you would have to pay 30%. There are usually deductibles required each year and you can also expect to pay co-pays which are often larger than in an HMO.

FFS – Fee-For-Service. The Fee-for-Service plans are offered nationwide and all federal employees have access to them. The line between a PPO and Fee-for-Service plan is fairly blurry. Like the PPO, you can choose your provider from an approved list. Your reimbursement is normally 80% of covered expenses which are considered reasonable and customary - as determined in the contract between the provider and the insurance company.

Comparing an HMO to a PPO or FFS; you have less flexibility and more restrictions in an HMO which results in lower premiums, but possibly higher out-of-pocket expenses. The more choices and control you have, the more it costs you. Should you choose a traditional plan? Much of this decision is driven by how healthy you and your family are. Your health will be a guiding factor in choosing the best coverage for you. Traditional coverage is designed for people with fairly significant health issues. If you have a chronic condition, see a specialist more than 3 times a year, and are on several on-going medications, then a traditional plan may be for you. Although there are usually higher premiums associated with traditional plans, you will also be likely to have more of your health expenses covered during the year. As with all of the health plans offered through FEHB, there are annual out-of-pocket maximums that limit how much you would have to pay in any given year.

Consumer-driven Health plans: These are recommended for those who have fewer health issues than those mentioned for traditional coverage. You might have a minor ongoing condition such as allergies or acid reflux for which you take one or two prescriptions occasionally. If you see a specialist, it might only be once or twice per year. Consumer-driven Health plans typically have a set amount of coverage that they pay before you are required to pay anything - a reverse deductible if you will. As an example, the insurer might pay the first $2,500 in expenses on a family's coverage. You would then be responsible for the next $1,500 and then the insurance company would pick up 90% of the charges and you would be responsible for 10%, up to an out-of-pocket maximum of $6,000. Any amounts you do not use out of the insurer's first $2,500 can be rolled over to the next year - provided you stay in the same health plan. So, if you only needed $2,000 of coverage this year and stayed in the same plan, next year, the insurer would pay the first $3,000 of your expenses ($500 from this year + $2,500 for next year).

These plans are for those who are generally healthy:

HDHP – High-deductible health plans. High-Deductible Health plan is a fairly new offering for the federal government. Less than 2% of federal employees are enrolled in these plans. We believe this is not because they are not viable options, but because employees simply don't understand the benefits. If you do not have any known medical issues and only go to the doctor for routine physicals or the occasional flu, and you don't have any ongoing prescription needs, this might be a great choice for you. High-Deductible Health plan can be expected to have lower premiums with higher deductibles. For any of you who remember what they used to call catastrophic insurance where you only had coverage for a major health event, but you could afford to pay for other day-to-day health care expenses - that is essentially what High-Deductible Health plan does.

HSA – Health Savings Account. The High-Deductible Health plan comes with a Health Savings Account. The HSA associated with the High-Deductible Health plan is different from the Flexible Savings Account (FSA). The biggest complaint about the FSA is that it is a use-it-or-lose-it option. The HSA funds roll over from one year to the next - regardless of whether you stay in a Deductible Health plan or not. Another difference is that the HSA funds earn tax-free interest where FSA funds do not. I'll cover more on FSAs later in this chapter. The funds are completely portable, meaning that if you retire or leave federal service, the funds are yours to take with you and spend on health care expenses in the future. The custodian of the HSA will provide you with a debit card which you can use to pay deductibles, co-pays and other health-related expenses. You can continue in a High-Deductible Health plan in retirement until you reach age 65 and become eligible for Medicare. The funds you accumulate in your HSA during your working years can be utilized for health care expenses in retirement - including premiums on your federal employee health benefits after age 65.

The HSA acts as a healthcare IRA. The funds are even inheritable by your heirs. How do you get funds into your HSA? There are two ways. The first is to contribute funds each month. This can come directly out of your checking account to go, pre-tax, into the HSA. The second way is that the insurer gives back a portion of the premium you pay directly into the HSA. You receive a rebate from the premiums you pay, actually reducing your overall health care costs. You must be in a High-Deductible Health plan to have an HSA. The only exclusions from participating in the HSA are:

- You cannot be enrolled in Medicare.
- You cannot be enrolled in a non-OPM health plan.
- You cannot have accessed benefits through the VA in the past three months.
- You cannot be enrolled in Tri-Care or Tri-Care for Life.
- It will limit how you can participate in an FSA (you can't contribute to the FSA for health care expenses, but you are still allowed to use the FSA for dental and vision).

Some common expenses you can pay out of your HSA include:

- Out-of-pocket expenses like deductibles and co-pays
- Dental expenses
- Vision exams
- Contacts, glasses
- Hearing aids and batteries
- Chiropractors
- Acupuncture
- Qualified long-term care premiums

Using the HSA's tax-free capabilities is the only way to get a federal tax break on your long-term care premiums. SO WHAT'S THE DIFFERENCE? We've talked about types of plans and how your health can help determine your best option, but what about things like levels of service and how much control you have over your own healthcare? The following chart shows four areas you should consider when making your decision.

	HDHP	PPO/FFS	HMO
Red Tape/ Paperwork	Lots	Some	Almost None
Emphasis on Keeping You Out of the Hospital	Cost incentives	Pre-approval	Non-hospital Treatment first
Choices of Doctors, Hospitals and Other providers	Some are net-work only; others pay something for out-of-network	In network Reduces cost; Out-of-network provides Increase costs	Must use in-network providers; no coverage for out-of-network
Use Case Management	Limited	Limited	Substantial

In terms of paperwork, an HMO is the easiest to deal with, while the High-Deductible Health plan involves more paperwork and pre-authorizations. The High-Deductible Health plan provides incentives to the plan participant in taking responsibility for their care, while the PPO and Fee-for-Service plans require pre-authorization, and the HMO endorses non-hospital treatments. All three types of plans require you to utilize their preferred providers to different degrees. It's your responsibility to understand what is required by the plan in order to avoid unnecessary out-of-pocket expenses for yourself.

Each of the High-Deductible Health plans and the PPO/FFS have limited case management capabilities. This means you will be responsible for managing more of your overall health care. For example, if you're having surgery, you'll need to be sure that not only the hospital and surgeon are on your insurer's preferred provider list, but that the anesthesiologist and any other medical professionals who might consult on your case are on that preferred list. The strength of HMO's is their case management ability. You don't have to be concerned about whether a specialist is on a preferred provider list because if your primary care physician has referred them, they have to be within the system. This is done to contain costs.

Speaking of costs, how important is cost to you? Of course, we all want to pay as little as possible for health insurance, but is it your most important concern? While you are working, your share of the insurance premium is paid with pre-tax dollars—called premium conversion. Once you retire, you no longer receive this benefit and must pay your premiums with after-tax dollars. The federal government continues to pay their proportionate share, approximately 72%, for both you and your spouse even after retirement. This is one of the best benefits you get for your years of public service. Your spouse can continue on your coverage as long as you live, but if you want to ensure that their coverage continues even if you pass away first, you'll want to be sure and take a survivorship benefit on your federal annuity for them.

This election at retirement allows you and your spouse to be covered by federal health benefits as long as you both live, with the federal government paying 72% of your premium and you paying 28%. Often two federal employees will be married to each other and each take self-only health coverage. The premiums for two self-only policies are less than family coverage. This seems like a cost-effective plan. However, keep in mind that each employee has to meet the plan's maximum out-of-pocket limit if there are two separate plans. This is particularly of interest as employees/retirees age and tend to have higher overall health care expenses. You are eligible to continue your health benefits in retirement as long as you retire on an immediate annuity and have been enrolled in the FEHB for at least five years either as an employee or family member. You do not have to be enrolled in the same health plan the entire five years, but continuously enrolled in any FEHB plan.

A common misconception is that your spouse has to be enrolled for five years prior to your retirement. This is not true. As long as your spouse has other coverage, they can enroll in your plan either after a life-changing event or during any open season. A pitfall to avoid here is that if your spouse continues to work after you retire and keeps their own health coverage thinking they'll get on your plan when they retire and the federal retiree passes away before the spouse has a chance to retire. The spouse loses the access to those health benefits because they were not covered by the FEHB at the time of the retiree's passing. Even if you take the survivor benefit to enable your spouse to continue health benefits if you pass away first, and if the spouse is not covered by FEHB on the day you die; they are unable to get FEHB coverage. Your overall health care expenses include more than just your share of the premium. You also have to take into consideration what your maximum deductibles could be, as well as any co-pays for doctors, hospitalization and prescriptions. In the case of the High-Deductible Health plan, you also get a rebate from the insurance company, so you get to deduct that amount from your overall expenses.

Take a Look at the following illustration comparing out-of-pocket expenses for an employee insuring self only:

Self Only	HDHP	Standard
Limit state in Plan's Summary of Benefits	$5,000	$4,500
Deductible	Included	$350
Hospital, Physician, Drug Co-pays	Included	$2,560
Specialty Drug	Included	$4,000
Premium Minus Savings Account	$88	$1,992
Actual Limit to You	$5,088	$13,402

As you can see in this table, it's possible to pay much higher expenses in a standard level plan than the high-deductible health plan, especially if you have to meet the full deductible in each plan.

Dental and Vision

In 2006, the federal government added separate dental and vision benefits to your health benefit offerings. Some health plans include a small provision for dental coverage, but it is usually limited so you might want to have additional coverage. The coverage is available to all current and retired federal employees through FEDVIP. It is offered on a group basis which reduces the cost of the premiums, but the government does not subsidize any portion of the premium. One of the issues with the FEHB is that you must choose between self or family coverage. If you are married with no children, you pay the same amount as the co-worker who is married with four children. The dental and vision programs allow you to choose between self only, self + one, and self + family to make the premiums fairer. As in the health plans, pre-existing conditions are covered, although you'll want to check the limitations for things like orthodontics, crowns and bridge work. You also get to pay your premiums with pre-tax dollars just like your health insurance. You can choose dental only, vision only, both, or neither. NOTE: You do not have to be enrolled in the FEHB to participate - although you must be eligible for the FEHB.

The dental and vision coverage are the secondary payers if you have coverage under your FEHB. An example is, if available, your health coverage would pay first, then your FEDVIP coverage and finally, if you're enrolled in the FSA; you could use those funds to pay any remaining amounts due. When comparing dental benefits, you're looking to find the best coverage that used in combination with your health coverage and FSA, will provide the most benefit for you and your family.

FSA – Flexible Savings Account

The Flexible Savings Account is not actually part of your health insurance coverage, but the open season is the same as the health plans. You must re-enroll and choose your contribution amounts to the FSA each year. You may contribute up to $5,000 each year in pre-tax dollars to be used for health expenses. Depending on your tax bracket, this effectively allows you to get a 20-40% discount on health-related expenses because you are paying for those expenses with pre-tax dollars. You can use the funds to pay medical expenses such as co-pays, deductibles, dental and vision care, prescription and non-prescription drugs. Remember, your ability to contribute to the health portion is limited to use for dental and vision care if you are enrolled in the High-Deductible Health plan and the HSA. You can also set aside $5,000 in pre-tax dollars to pay for dependent care for children under the age of 13, parents or other relatives dependent on you for their care and listed on your tax return. The biggest complaint about the FSA is that if you don't use your contributions from the previous year by March 15, you lose them. You can drive down the street in early March and in any drug store you will see signs like "Spend your FSA $ here". You can spend left-over funds on band-aids, aspirin, contact lenses and solution among other things. You can get more specific information on how your FSA dollars can be spent at www.fsafeds.com.

Final Considerations

Choosing Your Plan: If you're going to compare the health plans available in your area, you'll want to start by choosing from the HMO/PPO/Fee-for-Service options and choose which ones you want to review. Can you live with the limits of an HMO? If you want a little more control, you might move toward a consumer-driven health plan or High-Deductible Health plan. How healthy are you and the members of your family? Do you have any specialist needs? Remember, the healthier you are, the lower options of the consumer-driven and High-Deductible Health plans become. You'll also want to consider what health services are important to you. Think about well child check-ups, chiropractic care, mental health, emergency services, preventative screenings and hospitalization. There are probably only a few of these services that are important to you, and these needs will change over the years; which is why you'll want to review your health coverage at least every three years.

The plan documents that outline each insurer's coverage can be intimidating. Although they are supposed to make choosing a plan easier, they often serve the opposite purpose. They appear overwhelming and, as a result, many employees simply stay with the same plan from year-to-year without evaluating whether it's still the best coverage for them. Let's take a closer look: OPM did a great thing for you in terms of the plan documents. Any insurer who provides coverage under the federal health plan must organize their plan documents in the same format. This means that all the plans will have similar features in approximately the same place in each document. An example: any plan changes are documented in section 2. Even if you don't plan to change health plans, you should always look at this section for the plan you're currently in, so you're aware of any changes to the plan for the upcoming year. Detailed benefit descriptions always appear in section 5. You'll look here if you have a chronic condition and want to see exactly how it's handled. A summary of all plan benefits always appears in section 11.

Medicare

We'll close out this chapter with a short overview of Medicare and how it integrates with your federal employee health benefits. One of the most common questions we hear is what to do about Medicare and my federal employee health benefits when I turn 65. There are four components to Medicare.

Medicare Part A

Medicare Part A is the hospitalization coverage portion of Medicare and is free to anyone who has paid into the Medicare system for at least 40 quarters (or ten years). Because all federal employees were required to begin paying into Medicare in March of 1986, even if you're in CSRS, you should be covered here. Because it is free to you - you've paid in 1.45% while you're working - you'll want to sign up for this coverage at age 65. Your FEHB insurer wants you to sign up as well, because it helps take some of the burden off them. You'll sign up for Medicare Part A when you turn 65. You have 7 months-that's three months before your 65th birthday, the month of your birthday, and three months after your 65th birthday to enroll. Whether you're still working or not, you'll want to sign up for Medicare Part A, because you do not pay anything for this coverage. If you are still working at age 65, your FEHB will remain the primary payer until you retire, when Medicare will take over as the primary payer.

Medicare Part B

Medicare Part B has a cost of $96.40 per month and if you opt for this coverage at age 65 (or when you retire, whichever is later), it becomes your primary insurer and your FEHB acts as a Medicare Supplement. If your modified adjusted gross annual income is greater than $85,000, your premium increases on a sliding scale. This is known as means testing. If you have the means to pay more - you're charged more for Medicare Part B. Many federal employees question whether they need Medicare Part B. Keep in mind that unless you're turning 65 soon; much of what you're reading here could change by the time you get there.

The general pros and cons of choosing Medicare Part B are as follows: on the positive side, you'll have broader access and stand to have a greater portion of your health care expenses paid for. If you're in an HMO within your FEHB, you won't have to worry about those out-of-network costs being covered. Medicare would pick that up. If you choose Medicare Part B, you will pay at least $96.40 more per month in premiums (in addition to your then current FEHB premiums). Health care expenses for a couple enrolled in Blue Cross Blue Shield would be more than $7,000 per year before ever going to the doctor. If you're healthy, you could save about $2,300 per year by simply keeping your FEHB only.

The downside of Medicare is that if you choose Medicare Part B, Medicare becomes the primary payer (they pay the first dollar expenses). Having Medicare become the primary payer means that you have to go to a physician who accepts Medicare. Many physicians are no longer accepting Medicare because it is a time consuming process to file the paperwork, which results in lower payouts than the typical insurer would pay and it often takes longer for Medicare to pay them. You may also have to give up the physician you've gone to for years if you choose the Medicare Part B option. Unfortunately, more and more doctors are not taking Medicare. If you are already retired when you turn 65, the rules are the same for enrolling in Medicare Part B as for Part A. However, you may still be working at age 65 so that, hopefully, you won't have to make the Medicare Part B decision until up to 8 months after you retire. If you do not enroll during this timeframe, you may still enroll during any open season which runs from January 1 to March 31 each year. However, you will incur a 10% penalty for each year past the enrollment deadline. You'll want to carefully evaluate your Medicare Part B options at age 65, so hopefully, you won't have to reconsider it in the future. The 10%/year penalty increases your premium permanently. Since most federal employees are satisfied with their FEHB coverage, they simply keep that coverage at age 65.

Medicare Part C

Medicare Part C is also known as Medicare Advantage and acts like an HMO for Medicare participants. You must have Medicare Part A and Part B to participate in Medicare Part C.

Medicare Part D

Medicare Part D is the prescription drug program enacted by President Bush in 2003. Depending on the prescription drug provisions of your FEHB, you may not need this coverage. As long as you have some prescription coverage within your FEHB, you are allowed to pick up Medicare Part D during any open enrollment without a penalty.

Summary

As complicated as this part of your package may seem, understanding your options here can save you thousands of dollars over your career and into retirement. The government health plan is among the best in the country because of the variety of options you have to choose from each year, and the fact that they subsidize your premiums by 72% for life. You can see what an important benefit the FEHB provides in your overall benefits and retirement package.

CHAPTER SEVEN:

Retirement Systems Explained

I will use this chapter to discuss the basics of the three retirement systems (CSRS, Civil Service Off-Set and FERS). To start, let's cover the two most common questions I hear from employees about federal retirement:

1. Should I buy back my military time?
2. What is the number in the lower right-hand corner of my paystub?

Civil Service (CSRS) employees were hired prior to January 1, 1984, or had at least 5 years of CSRS service and returned to work between the years of 1984 and 1987. A Civil Service employee could fully retire at age 55 with at least 30 years of service. If the employee worked past the 30-year minimum, he or she could earn a higher annuity (pension) in retirement. With 40 years of service, CSRS employees could earn as much as 80% of their average high three consecutive years of base pay as a pension. The CSRS employee pays 7% of his or her income toward CSRS retirement. CSRS employees did not pay into Social Security. Those employees who earned their 40 quarters of Social Security credits prior to their federal service or by working a second job could earn a Social Security check on top of their pension checks. However, because of the Windfall Elimination Provision, their Social Security checks would be cut in half. The government viewed a CSRS employee as double dipping by getting a full pension and Social Security from the government. This provision has been challenged by CSRS employees but, as of today, it is still in effect.

One important choice or option the CSRS employee has pertains to the Survivor Benefit. A Survivor Benefit is a benefit paid to an employee's surviving spouse in the event of the employee's death. A CSRS employee can elect as much as 50% of the employee's pension check as a Survivor Benefit. This election will reduce their monthly check by 10% while they are living, and pay 50% to a surviving spouse for the remainder of their lifetime. They can also select any amount smaller than 50% and will see a corresponding reduction in their pension check depending on what they choose. There are instances where the employee's spouse will not need a Survivor Benefit. It could be that the spouse has their own pension that will pay more than the Survivor Benefit. Regardless of the reason, they can elect zero Survivor Benefit. If they elect this option, the spouse will have to sign and notarize forms within the retirement package confirming this decision. A very important issue to keep in mind when electing a Survivor Benefit as a CSRS employee is health insurance.

An employee's spouse is eligible to maintain health insurance in retirement as long as the employee elected a Survivor Benefit for their spouse. This means, if an employee does not elect a Survivor Benefit, they will not be eligible for health coverage under the federal health plan. CSRS employees who want the health coverage for their spouse, but also want the biggest pension check they can get, should elect a $3,600 annual Survivor Benefit. This election will allow the spouse access to health coverage, but the annual amount is so small it will have a very minimal effect on the employee's pension check. With $3,600 annually, there is enough of a check coming to the spouse to cover the health insurance premiums. In the event of the employee's death, it is much easier on the spouse if the pension check will cover the cost of the health insurance, preventing the spouse from having to remember to write a check each month. A retiree may elect less than

$3,600 annually. We only suggest the amount that is currently needed to help cover health insurance costs.

CSRS/OFF-SET employees are employees who had 5 years of federal service prior to 1983, separated for at least one year and then returned to federal service in 1984 or later. The government required every federal employee after 1984 to pay Social Security. Because of this requirement, CSRS/OFF-SET was created. We will not bore you with the details but will try to help you understand how it affects your pension check. CSRS/OFF-SET is a CSRS employee. The only difference is you pay into Social Security and the regular CSRS doesn't. Let's look at an example. If Bob retires at age 55 with 30 years of service as a CSRS/OFF-SET employee, he will receive the full 56.25% pension that is allowed for a normal CSRS employee. When Bob turns 62 and becomes eligible for Social Security his pension check will be offset by his Social Security check.

Pension check at 55	$2,125.00
Social Security Check at 62	$1,000.0

Retirement Income at 62:

Pension Check	$1,125.00
SSI Check	$1,000.00

In a nutshell, you get the exact same monthly income as a regular CSRS employee. The only difference is that at age 62 the income will come from two sources instead of one. FERS employees hired January 1, 1984 and after are FERS employees. Many people ask us why a second retirement system was created. No one will ever know the entire reasoning behind the government's decision to change systems. However, we will show you how FERS works and then you can make your own assessment as to the motivations behind the creation of this system. FERS employees pay very little toward their retirement compared to CSRS employees. The CSRS employee paid 7% toward retirement where a FERS employee will only pay .08% (not even 1%) toward retirement. It is also important to look at the differences in pension amounts between a FERS and a CSRS employee. A CSRS employee after 30 years and at age 55 will earn a pension check for life of 56.25% of their highest three years of salary. A FERS employee will only earn 30% after 30 years of service and reaching their minimum retirement age. We have listed the minimum retirement ages with 30 years of service below:

If you were born before 1948 55

In 1948	55 and 2 months
In 1949	55 and 4 months
In 1950	55 and 6 months
In 1951	55 and 8 months
In 1952	55 and 10 months
In 1953-1964	56
In 1965	56 and 2 months
In 1967	56 and 6 months
In 1968	56 and 8 months
In 1969	56 and 10 months
In 1970 and after	57

You can also retire with less than 30 years of service and your minimum retirement age with:

- 20 years of service at age 60 - 20% pension (1% per year of service)
- 5 years of service at age 62 - 5% pension (1% per year of service).

FERS employees pay into Social Security as well.

Social Security is the second piece of the FERS retirement plan. One thing you may notice about the FERS retirement system is that you are eligible to retire at ages under 62 before you would be eligible for Social Security. How can FERS employees afford to retire without getting their Social Security checks? The answer is the FERS Special Supplement. Very few employees are aware of this program. The FERS Special Supplement is money every FERS employee needs to be aware of. Let's look at Bob, a FERS employee. He is retiring with 30 years of service at age 56. He is not eligible to draw Social Security until age 62. Under the FERS Special Supplement he is entitled to receive a check from the Office of Personnel Management equaling 75% of whatever his Social Security benefit would be at age 62. If Bob's age is 62, his Social Security benefit is $1,200, therefore his FERS Special Supplement would equal $900. Bob would get this check from age 56 to age 62. Once Bob becomes eligible for Social Security, the supplement is stopped and Social Security starts sending his normal check. CAUTION: It is very important that the employee understands that you have to reach your minimum retirement age and either 30 years of service, or age 60 with 20 years of service to qualify for the Special Supplement. Some agencies are offering Early Outs. If you have not met the minimum retirement age and years of service, you will not get the supplement. This can make a significant difference in your evaluation of taking an Early Out or not.

Should I Buy Back My Military Time?

In most cases, the answer is yes. Unless you are receiving a military retirement pension or insurance benefits, you should consider buying the time. The cost of doing so will usually be covered in less than 2 years by the increased pension amount. FERS employees with military service BEFORE January 1, 1957 will receive credit for their military time for annuity computations and no buy-back deposit is required. The FERS deposit is 3% of basic pay plus a variable market rate interest may be charged. Military deposits must be completed before you retire. For example, let's say Bob served 4 years in the Army. At $10,000 per year, his base pay totaled $40,000. Buying this time back will require a deposit of 3%, or $1,200 plus any applicable interest. This can be done in a lump sum or arranged to be taken through payroll deductions, as long as it is completed prior to retirement. Adding 4 years of service will add 4% to his FERS retirement pension. Since Bob's high-three salary is $50,000, 4% will add $2,000 per year to his retirement pension, or $167 each month. That will repay Joe's buy-back deposit in only 8 months. As a general rule, all honorable active duty military service is potentially creditable under FERS.

What is the number in the lower right-hand corner of my Postal paystub? This is the amount you have contributed to your retirement. CSRS employees contribute 7% of each check, while the FERS employees put in .08% of their pay. You will find the bi-weekly amount on your paystub next to the Retire (#) designation. This amount accumulates all year and is added to the total at the bottom of your paystub each January. Here's what you need to know about this money:

- You are guaranteed to get it back in retirement.
- You have paid taxes on it when it was taken out, so it will be tax-free when it is given back.
- You have an option to take it ALL as a lump sum at retirement in place of receiving any additional pension. If you do not choose the lump-sum option, a portion will be returned to you each year tax-free as part of your pension, and the amount and number of years will be based on the amount of your contributions and your average life-expectancy at the time of retirement.

In other words, if when you retire you have an anticipated life expectancy of 10 years, they will take your total contribution, divided by 120 months, and that amount will be included as part of your pension payments each year for the first 120 months of retirement. Part of your monthly pension check will be tax-free for the first 10 years. If you die prior to receiving the full reimbursement of your contributions, the unpaid balance will be paid as a lump-sum benefit to your beneficiaries. If you live beyond your life expectancy, your pension will remain the same, but it will no longer have the tax-free portion from your contributions. This has very small implications for the FERS or CSRS Off-Set retiree, since the bulk of their contributions were paid to Social Security, and not into the retirement fund.

But for the Civil Service retiree, this can have a huge impact in the later stages of retirement.

Look at this example:

Frank is a CSRS employee who retires at age 67 after 42 years with the government.

- His retirement contributions and interest total $112,000.
- At retirement, OPM determines his life-expectancy to be 7 years (84 months).
- His monthly pension is 80% of his $64,000 high-three base salary, or $48,000/year.
- His contributions ($112,000) will be returned to him as part of his pension for the next seven years at $16,000/year ($1,333/month).

Frank's pension will be $4,000/month, but because part of that is repayment of his contributions, he will owe taxes on less than $2,700 per month. Frank thinks this is GREAT... until he outlives his life expectancy. After age 74, his contributions are fully repaid, and he now owes taxes on the whole amount he receives. Because of taxes, his check will, without warning, be reduced by $300-500 per month. Your repayment schedule will be set at the time you retire based on the current average life-expectancy tables and your contributions.

CHAPTER EIGHT:

Maxing Your Retirement Income

I will use this chapter to address some important questions about the two primary retirement systems: Civil Service Retirement System (CSRS), and Federal Employee Retirement System (FERS). With a very few exceptions, CSRS employees are those hired prior to January 1, 1984, or those with at least 5 years of CSRS service who left and returned to work before January 1, 1988. FERS employees are those hired after January 1, 1984. The CSRS pension grows by 2% each year up to 42 years of service which, on a $52,000 annual salary, is about $80 in additional monthly retirement income for every year of additional work.

The FERS employee pension will grow by 1% each year, adding about $40/month in retirement income. In addition, the FERS employee who delays drawing Social Security until age 66 will generally add $300-400/month in retirement income. Working 2 or 3 extra years also gives time to add to TSP and other investment funds, which will increase future income. Working into your retirement years may not be your first choice, but sometimes it simply becomes a necessity. No matter what your situation, the closer we get to retirement, the more important it becomes to get the most out of every dollar. I have already suggested that the best way to grow your TSP account is to contribute the amount needed to receive the 5% match. Don't miss out on free money, it's probably the only free money you will ever receive in your lifetime! When taking the funds out you need to seek the highest return with little or no risk.

During your separation and retirement process, Shared Services will offer you two options for distributing funds out of your TSP account. First, you can cash it out and pay the total amount owed in taxes in one year. Depending upon the TSP value, this can put you into a higher tax bracket and further reduce any gains. High taxes and lump sum can negatively affect your retirement income.

The second option they can offer you is to sell your TSP. They don't call it that. They call it an annuity, but the reality of the second choice is to sell your accumulated TSP funds in exchange for a monthly income. The federal annuity will pay a lifetime income of approximately $600 each month for every $100,000 in your TSP. To a retiring employee faced with a significant reduction in income, and compared to Option 1, the extra dollars from the annuity may look attractive but read the fine print because this can be a very costly decision. In effect, you lose all rights to the principle. Your payments are locked in with only cost-of-living increases. There is no death benefit. You may choose a reduced monthly payment and select a survivor option. However, there is no guarantee the total payout will match or exceed your beginning balance, and all payments stop with the death of the recipients. There is no inheritance to pass on to family members, and no final expense fund. There is no provision to access a larger portion of the money should funds be needed for nursing home care, terminal illness or other life events. The federal annuity essentially pays out interest in the form of monthly payments and keeps all the principle. What's my recommendation? Do not choose this option!

There is a third option available. As with all employer sponsored plans, the TSP funds can be rolled-over to your own IRA. There are many IRA plans available and dozens of companies outside the government that will help you in making a decision.

Sorting through all of the options can be a daunting task. The key is to seek the advice of an expert. You should make the effort to consult with someone who specializes in this field. When it comes to financial investing it is important to read the fine print and do your homework. It is best to get a couple of different opinions. Every advisor is going to have their own spin on things so it is wise to look at more than one option. With the unstable market we have experienced over the past several years, you will want to find out the history of the advisor and the types of financial products they provide. Does this investment they are recommending have exposure to market risk? Can the gains be locked in each year? What are the fees if any? These are just some of the questions that need to be asked.

There are primarily three investment options you have available for your IRA. Each of these options has positives and negatives. If an advisor tells you they have an investment option with no downside, put your hands over your ears, start humming and run! You know this cannot be true. With no order of preference, these are your most common options.

1. IRA/bank CD. The upside? Very safe. You are covered up to $250,000 by FDIC, so there is no way you can lose your funds as long as the account is titled correctly. Make sure that if you have more than one account with the same bank, they are each titled differently. Most are not aware of the fact that you can lose money if a bank fails regardless of the FDIC coverage. In order to have $250,000 FDIC coverage for each account at the same bank they must each be titled with a different name. Is a bank CD really a good place for long term retirement investing or distribution? Not in my opinion. A bank CD is a good place for temporarily parking money, but not for retirement assets.

2. Brokerage or managed assets such as mutual funds, bond funds, stocks, ETFs etc... This is where your greatest growth potential is found. Notice I said "potential". I didn't say "guarantee". As long as you understand the fees and risks associated with these

types of investments, than it is a viable option. Just remember that <u>you</u> are shouldering the risk, not the broker, not the fund manager, not the brokerage firm. YOU!

3. Insurance company. The insurance company is going to offer you an annuity. If you want guarantees with no market risk, then you will want to stay with a fixed or fixed indexed annuity. These annuities have certain caps and limitations as to the upside one can earn, but for the risk-averse investor; in my opinion it is the best way to go.

CHAPTER NINE:

Roth TSP vs. Traditional Roth

Tax free income. Those three words just make me warm and fuzzy all over. Nothing like getting one over on the IRS! Tax free income? Are you kidding me? Is there really a true tax free income available in this country? The answer is yes. In fact there are two tax free incomes that we can take advantage of. How about life insurance? That's right, life insurance can provide tax free income. The proceeds to the beneficiary(s) are totally 100% tax free! You may say; well, what good does that do me? I'll be dead and gone. The fact is, you can borrow against the cash value in a life insurance policy and the income is tax free. I have structured many life insurance policies to maximize the cash value while minimizing the death benefit so as to provide tax free income in retirement. I use life insurance to solve estate tax issues as well. But since this chapter is about Roth, let's move on.

Let me make one thing clear before we get deep into this discussion. The Roth TSP Is NOT a traditional Roth. I will take some time to review the traditional Roth so you can learn the distinct differences between the two. The Roth IRA was established by the Taxpayer Relief Act of 1997 (Public Law 105-34) and named for its chief legislative sponsor, Senator William Roth of Delaware. In contrast to a traditional IRA, contributions to a Roth IRA are not tax-deductible. Withdrawals are generally tax-free, but not always and not without certain stipulations (i.e., tax free for principal withdrawals and the owner's age must be at least 59½ for tax free withdrawals on the growth portion above principal). An advantage of the Roth IRA over a traditional IRA is that there are fewer withdrawal restrictions and requirements. Transactions inside an account (including capital gains, dividends, and interest) do not incur a current tax liability.

Advantages:

- Direct contributions to a Roth IRA may be withdrawn tax free at any time.
- Rollover, converted (before age 59½) contributions held in a Roth IRA may be withdrawn tax and penalty free after the "seasoning" period (currently 5 years).
- Earnings may be withdrawn tax and penalty free after the seasoning period if the condition of age 59½ (or other qualifying condition) is also met.

This differs from a traditional IRA where all withdrawals are taxed as Ordinary Income, and a penalty applies for withdrawals before age 59½. In contrast, capital gains on stocks or other securities held in a regular taxable account for at least a year would be taxed at the lower long-term capital gain rate, which is currently 15%. This potentially higher tax rate for withdrawals of capital gains from a traditional IRA is a quid pro quo for the deduction taken against ordinary income when putting money into the IRA.

If there is money in the Roth IRA due to conversion from a traditional IRA, the Roth IRA owner may withdraw up to the total of the converted amount without penalty, as long as the "seasoning" period (currently five years) has passed on the converted funds. Up to a lifetime maximum of $10,000 in earnings withdrawals are considered qualified (tax-free) if the money is used to acquire a principal residence for a first time buyer. This house must be acquired by the Roth IRA owner, their spouse, or their lineal ancestors and descendants. The owner or qualified relative who receives such a distribution must not have owned a home in the previous 24 months. Contributions may be made to a Roth IRA even if the owner participates in a qualified retirement plan such as a 401(k). (Contributions may be made to a traditional IRA in this circumstance, but they may not be tax deductible.)

If a Roth IRA owner dies and his/her spouse becomes the sole beneficiary of that Roth IRA while also owning a separate Roth IRA, the spouse is permitted to combine the two Roth IRAs into a single plan without penalty.

If the Roth IRA owner expects that the tax rate applicable to withdrawals from a traditional IRA in retirement will be higher than the tax rate applicable to the funds earned to make the Roth IRA contributions before retirement, then there may be a tax advantage to making contributions to a Roth IRA over a traditional IRA or similar vehicle while working. There is no current tax deduction, but money going into the Roth IRA is taxed at the taxpayer's current marginal tax rate, and will not be taxed at the expected higher future effective tax rate when it comes out of the Roth IRA. Assets in the Roth IRA can be passed on to heirs.

The Roth IRA does not require distributions based on age. All other tax-deferred retirement plans, including the related Roth TSP, require withdrawals to begin by April 1 of the calendar year after the owner reaches age 70½. If one does not need the money and wants to leave it to their heirs, this is a great way to accumulate tax free income. Beneficiaries who inherited Roth IRAs are subject to the minimum distribution rules.

Roth IRAs have a higher "effective" contribution limit than traditional IRAs, since the nominal contribution limit is the same for both traditional and Roth IRAs; but the post-tax contribution in a Roth IRA is equivalent to a larger pre-tax contribution in a traditional IRA that will be taxed upon withdrawal. For example, a contribution of the 2008 limit of $5,000 to a Roth IRA may be equivalent to a traditional IRA contribution of $6667 (assuming a 25% tax rate at both contribution and withdrawal). In 2008, one cannot contribute $6667 to a traditional IRA due to the contribution limit, so the post-tax Roth contribution may be larger.

On estates large enough to be subject to estate taxes, a Roth IRA can reduce estate taxes since tax dollars have already been subtracted. A traditional IRA is valued at the pre-tax level for estate tax purposes.

Disadvantages: Funds that reside in a Roth IRA cannot be used as collateral for a loan per current IRS rules and therefore cannot be used for financial leveraging or a cash management tool for investment purposes. Contributions to a Roth IRA are not tax deductible. By contrast, contributions to a traditional IRA are tax deductible (within income limits). Therefore, someone who contributes to a traditional IRA instead of a Roth IRA gets an immediate tax savings equal to the amount of the contribution multiplied by their marginal tax rate. Someone who contributes to a Roth IRA does not realize this immediate tax reduction. Also, by contrast, contributions to most employer sponsored retirement plans (such as a TSP, 401(k), 403(b), SIMPLE IRA or SEP IRA) are tax deductible with no income limits because they reduce a taxpayer's adjusted gross income.

Eligibility to contribute to a Roth IRA phases out at certain income limits. By contrast, contributions to most tax deductible employer sponsored retirement plans have no income limit. Contributions to a Roth IRA do not reduce a taxpayer's Adjusted Gross Income (AGI). By contrast, contributions to a traditional IRA, or most employer sponsored retirement plans, reduce a taxpayer's AGI. One of the key benefits of reducing one's AGI (aside from the obvious benefit of reducing taxable income) is that a taxpayer who is close to the threshold income of qualifying for some tax credits or tax deductions may be able to reduce their AGI below the threshold. By reducing below the threshold, he or she may become eligible to claim certain tax credits or tax deductions that may otherwise be phased out at the higher AGI had the taxpayer instead contributed to a Roth IRA. Likewise, the amount of those tax credits or tax deductions may be increased as the taxpayer slides down the phase out scale. Examples include the child tax credit, the earned income credit or the student loan interest deduction.

A taxpayer who chooses to make a Roth IRA contribution (instead of a traditional IRA contribution or tax deductible retirement account contribution) while in a moderate or high tax bracket will likely pay more income taxes on the earnings used to make the Roth IRA contribution. This is compared to the income taxes that would have been due to be paid on the funds that would have later been withdrawn from the traditional IRA, had the taxpayer made a traditional IRA contribution. This is because contributions to traditional IRAs or employer sponsored tax deductible retirement plans result in an immediate tax savings equal to the taxpayer's current marginal tax bracket multiplied by the amount of the contribution. It has been shown that many people have a lower income in retirement than during their working years, and thus end up in a lower tax bracket in retirement. This is another reason why withdrawals from a traditional IRA or tax deferred retirement plan in retirement are likely to result in a lower tax bill. The higher the taxpayer's marginal tax rate, the greater the disadvantage.

A taxpayer who pays state income taxes and who contributes to a Roth IRA (instead of a traditional IRA or a tax deductible employer sponsored retirement plan) will have to pay state income taxes on the amount contributed to the Roth IRA in the year the money is earned. However, if the taxpayer retires to a state with a lower income tax rate, or no income taxes; then the taxpayer will have given up the opportunity to avoid paying state income taxes altogether on the amount of the Roth IRA contribution by instead contributing to a traditional IRA or a tax deductible employer sponsored retirement plan. This is because when the contributions are withdrawn from the traditional IRA or tax deductible plan in retirement, the taxpayer will then be a resident of the low or no income tax state, and will have avoided paying the state income tax altogether as a result of moving to a different state before the income tax became due.

The perceived tax benefit may never be realized. In other words, one might not live to retirement or much beyond; in which case, the tax structure of a Roth only serves to reduce an estate that may not have been subject to tax. One must live until one's Roth IRA contributions have been withdrawn and exhausted to fully realize the tax benefit. Whereas, with a traditional IRA, tax might never be collected at all. In other words, if one dies prior to retirement with an estate below the tax threshold, or goes into retirement with income below the tax threshold (the beneficiary must be named in the appropriate IRA beneficiary form); a beneficiary inheriting the IRA solely through a will, would not be eligible for the estate tax exemption. Additionally, the beneficiary will be subject to income tax unless the inheritance is a Roth IRA. Heirs will have to pay taxes on withdrawals from traditional IRA assets they inherit, and must continue to take mandatory distributions (although it will be based on their life expectancy). It is also possible that tax laws may change by the time one reaches retirement age.

Congress may change the rules that currently allow for tax free withdrawal of Roth IRA contributions. Therefore, someone who contributes to a traditional IRA is guaranteed to realize an immediate tax benefit, whereas someone who contributes to a Roth IRA must wait for a number of years before realizing the tax benefit. That person assumes the risk that the rules might be changed during the interim. On the other hand, taxing earnings on an account which were promised to be untaxed may be seen as a violation of contract – individuals contributing to a Roth IRA now may in fact be saving themselves from new, possibly higher income tax obligations in the future. However, the federal government is not restricted by the Contract Clause of the U.S. Constitution that prohibits "Law[s] impairing the Obligation of Contracts". By its terms, this prohibition applies only to state governments.

Income limits:

Congress has limited who can contribute to a Roth IRA based upon income. A taxpayer can contribute the maximum amount listed at the top of the page only if their Modified Adjusted Gross Income (MAGI) is below a certain level (the bottom of the range shown below). Otherwise, a phase-out of allowed contributions runs proportionally throughout the MAGI ranges. Once MAGI hits the top of the range, no contribution is allowed at all; however, a minimum of $200 may be contributed as long as MAGI is below the top of the range (e.g. A single 40 year old with MAGI $124,999 may still contribute $200 to a Roth IRA vs. $30). Excess Roth IRA contributions may be redesigned into Traditional IRA contributions as long as the combined contributions do not exceed that tax year's limit.

The Roth IRA MAGI phase-out ranges for 2012 are:

- Single filers: Up to $110,000 (to qualify for a full contribution); $110,000–$125,000 (to be eligible for a partial contribution).
- Joint filers: Up to $173,000 (to qualify for a full contribution); $173,000–$183,000 (to be eligible for a partial contribution).
- Married filing separately (if the couple lived together for any part of the year): $0 (to qualify for a full contribution); $0–$10,000 (to be eligible for a partial contribution).

The lower number represents the point at which the taxpayer is no longer allowed to contribute the maximum yearly contribution. The upper number is the point as of which the taxpayer is no longer allowed to contribute at all. Note that people who are married and living together, but who file separately, are only allowed to contribute a relatively small amount. However, once a Roth IRA is established, the balance in the plan remains tax-sheltered, even if the taxpayer's income rises above the threshold. (The thresholds are just for annual eligibility to contribute, not for eligibility to maintain a Roth IRA.) This would be a wise move for retired people who have a comfortable asset base to pay the taxes. To be eligible, one must meet the earned income minimum requirement. In order to make a contribution, one must have taxable compensation (not taxable income from investments). If one makes only $2,000 in taxable compensation, one's maximum IRA contribution is $2,000.

Contribution limits:

Contributions to both a Roth IRA and a traditional IRA are limited to the total amount allowed for either ($5,000 for tax year 2012 - $6,000 if over 50 years of age). Generally, the contribution cannot exceed your earned income for the year in question. The one exception is for a "spousal IRA" where a contribution can be made for a spouse with little or no earned income provided the other spouse has sufficient earned income and the spouses file a joint tax return.

Conversion limit:

Through 2009, only taxpayers with MAGI less than $100,000 in the year of conversion and not married, filing separately were allowed to convert from a traditional IRA to a Roth IRA. TIPRA 2005 eliminated the MAGI limit and filing status restriction on conversions starting in 2010. Thus, regardless of income but subject to contribution limits, contributions can be made to a traditional IRA and then converted to a Roth IRA. The amount of the conversion that is taxable at the time of conversion equals the current value of the traditional IRA account minus nondeductible contributions to that account. A two-year spread rule applies to conversions made in 2010 and permitted the taxpayer to elect to include half the income in 2011 gross income and the other half in 2012 gross income. Taxable amounts related to conversions after 2010 must be included in gross income in the tax year that the distribution takes place. Since taxpayers may owe interest and penalties; if funds are removed from the traditional IRA account to pay the taxes, many advisors suggest using other funds to pay taxes on conversion income.

Distributions:

The principal of direct contributions may be withdrawn at any time without tax or penalty. Eligible (tax and penalty free) distributions of earnings must fulfill two requirements. First, the seasoning period of five years must have elapsed; and secondly, a justification must exist such as retirement or disability. The simplest justification is reaching 59 1/2 years of age, at which point qualified withdrawals may be made in any amount on any schedule. Becoming disabled or being a "first time" home buyer can provide justification for limited qualified withdrawals. Finally, although one can take distributions from a Roth IRA under the Substantially Equal Periodic Payments (SEPP) rule without paying a 10% penalty, any interest earned in the IRA will be subject to tax, a substantial penalty which forfeits the primary tax benefits of the Roth IRA.

Inherited Roth IRAs:

Transfers of Roth IRAs between spouses when one spouse dies – just like other IRAs – are tax-free, and the spousal beneficiary is free to make contributions and otherwise control the account. For estate tax purposes, if a Roth IRA is part of a descendant's estate that is valued under the taxable inheritance minimum; no estate tax needs to be paid. If the estate is larger than that, the Roth IRA will be taxable to beneficiaries (other than surviving spouses). Non-spouse beneficiaries are not allowed to make additional contributions to the inherited Roth IRA, or combine it with their own Roth IRA. In addition, the beneficiary may elect to choose from one of two methods of distribution. The first option is to receive the entire distribution by December 31 of the fifth year following the year of the IRA owner's death. The second option is to receive portions of the IRA as distributions over the life of the beneficiary, terminating upon the death of the beneficiary and passing on to a secondary beneficiary. For income tax purposes, distributions from Roth IRAs to beneficiaries are not taxable if the Roth IRA was established for at least five years before the distribution occurs.

The TSP began accepting Roth TSP contributions on May 7, 2012. Note that some participants have the ability to make Roth (after-tax) contributions to their TSP accounts. These contributions have to be held in a balance separate from traditional TSP contributions. This is because traditional and Roth contributions have different tax treatments, and the two types of contributions and their gains (or losses) have to be accounted for separately.

How does the Roth TSP compare to traditional TSP?

Greg Long, the executive director of the Federal Retirement Thrift Investment Board, says the one thing he wants all federal employee investors to understand is that "the Roth IRA and the Roth TSP are two very, very different things". He said he wished they had different names, because they are different in two very important ways.

First, the regular TSP, like the Roth TSP, is funded via payroll deduction. The money going into a regular TSP account is tax deferred. As Mr. Long says, it's a "pay me later" deal for Uncle Sam. The Roth TSP is totally different because it's funded with after-tax money. In other words, you pay the taxes on it before you invest. So when it comes out, it is all yours!

Secondly, and this is very important, there are no income limits on Roth TSP contributions. With a Roth IRA, if you make more than a certain amount ($183,000), you cannot contribute. But with the Roth TSP you can contribute after-tax money. So you could have a regular TSP account and a Roth TSP account at the same time. The only limit is the IRS limit on the amount an individual can contribute in one year. Mr. Long says he gets nervous when people fixate on the term "tax-free" with the Roth TSP. He said they need to study the option carefully and people "need to think long and hard" before choosing one option or the other.

Roth contributions are taken out of your paycheck after your income is taxed. When you withdraw funds from your Roth balance, you will receive your Roth contributions tax free since you have already paid taxes on the contributions. You also won't pay taxes on any earnings, as long as you're at least age 59 1/2 or disabled, and your withdrawal is made at least 5 years after the beginning of the year in which you made your first Roth contribution.

Traditional (pre-tax) contributions, which lower your current taxable income, give you a tax break today. They grow in your account tax-deferred, but when you withdraw your money, you pay taxes on both the contributions and their earnings. Here are some additional facts that you need to know: 1.) The 1% agency contribution does not vest for three years. 2.) New employees are automatically enrolled with a 3% Roth contribution. 3.) Congress may require force enrollment. 4.) Unlike the traditional Roth, the Roth TSP has RMD at age 70-1/2. Traditional Roth IRAs cannot be transferred to the Roth TSP.

Make sure you sign up for my free newsletter as I will include a segment in each issue to continue the Roth TSP updates as information becomes available. You can sign up for my newsletter by calling the office at 417-429-0331, or go to my website at www.federalemp.com

Go to this link to view a very informative video about the Roth TSP: https://www.tsp.gov/whatsnew/roth/index.shtml

Final Recommendations

The federal benefits and retirement package has four common problems that employees often don't discover until it's too late to change:

1. Retirement income has a higher tax liability than they anticipate.
2. With FEGLI, employees pay higher-than-market rates for life insurance, yet most are under-insured at their point of need.
3. Investment options in the TSP are low-return or high-risk, making it difficult to create enough retirement income.
4. Most federal employees will be forced into a lower standard of living and will be under-funded in retirement.

My experience in working with federal employees has taught me that no *one* solution is right for every situation and that, in most cases, we can only reduce, not eliminate, these four problems. The following suggestions, while general, when applied to specific situations have made the difference by hundreds of thousands of dollars for many federal employees. I understand your benefits package – its strengths and its weaknesses. I know how to help you get the most from your retirement plan, and show you choices that will allow you to take responsibility for your future. Remember, ultimately it's about you.

Minimize Tax Liability:

1. Take full advantage of the government-matched funds to your TSP contributions.
2. Open a Roth IRA (if you qualify) and maximize your contributions to it: $5,000 per year up to age 50, and $6,000 for those 50 and older. This earns tax-free interest and the benefits are substantial.
3. Rollover your TSP funds as quickly as possible - age 59 1/2 or separation from federal service, whichever comes first. Check my website for updated information (www.federalemp.com).

Resolve Insurance Issues:

1. Do a life insurance analysis.
2. Determine the amount of insurance needed, if any.
3. Carry only as much insurance as you need, and only for as long as you need it.
4. Make certain you qualify for new insurance before canceling any existing insurance.
5. Don't overpay. Insurance rates can vary. I can compare numerous companies for the best rates.
6. Participate in investment or savings programs that create adequate and accessible funds to reduce or eliminate the need for insurance altogether.

Reduce Investment Risk:

1. Grow your TSP through the matching funds and take advantage of guaranteed interest rates.
2. Open a Roth IRA with a guaranteed rate of interest and maximize your annual contribution.
3. At retirement or 59½ (whichever comes first), roll all available TSP funds into guaranteed growth annuities (my personal preference would be indexed annuities).

4. Compare before paying service charges or annual fees! The best programs available do not charge for using your money. In fact, many will pay you bonuses.

Increase Retirement Income:

1. Invest at least 10% of every dollar earned. For employees earning $52,000/year, that's $200/paycheck.
2. If you're just starting to invest and you're over 30, invest 15% ($300/paycheck).
3. If you're over 40 and just getting started, you will want to invest 15-20% ($300-400/paycheck).
4. Your first dollars should go into the TSP to take advantage of the matching funds.
5. Your next dollars should be directed into a Roth IRA with guaranteed interest. MAXIMIZE that fund every year!
6. Additional funds should go toward debt reduction, equity or purchasing hard assets or real property.
7. DO NOT use your retirement for speculation, no matter how sure it looks, or making loans to friends or family, no matter how urgent the need.

7 Bad TSP Investing Habits

We have all developed bad habits. I remember my Little League baseball days. Our coaches would consistently tell us not to develop a bad habit as it would relate to fielding the ball, batting stance, etc... We would spend hours practicing good habits while doing everything in our power not to gravitate to the bad ones. The same can be applied to TSP investing habits. Will you always get it right? Well, of course not. But you can learn to develop those habits that will give you the best shot at TSP success. The following 7 mistakes are the ones to avoid and will help put you in the position to maximize your TSP.

Bad Habit #1:

Not Contributing to the TSP. According to data provided by the Profit Sharing/401k Council of America, about 17% of all people eligible to participate in 401k-like plans such as the TSP don't. Are people finding other ways to invest their retirement savings? There's not enough data to know for sure, but it's safe to say that since retirement can seem so far away, it's easy to procrastinate. The fact is, many find that it is too late to do much about it. So, in many instances, what happens is we violate a key requirement of wealth accumulation: 1.) Sufficient time for money to compound. 2.) Adequate money exposed to compounding. 3.) A sufficient level earnings on those dollars over time. Time value of money. For FERS employees all the money contributed to their accounts vests immediately with the exception of the first 1% automatic agency contribution (taking three employment years to vest). This means the FERS employee earns 100% on his/her investment at the 5% contribution level. Where else can one invest like this?

Bad Habit #2:

As a FERS, Not Contributing 5%. Many FERS employees fail to contribute 5% to the TSP. Their reasons are numerous. When the federal government formed the FERS program, it was following suit with the private sector. This changed retirement systems from defined benefit systems (CSRS) to defined contribution systems (FERS). This change meant that FERS employees would establish more dependence upon the TSP investments than the CSRS employees would. Even though CSRS employees receive no matching government contributions to the TSP, it is still a good idea to contribute to the TSP.

Bad Habit #3:

Not Keeping the TSP-3 current. The TSP-3 is probably the most overlooked form in the entire benefit system. The TSP-3 form is what you complete to designate beneficiaries so the funds will be disbursed according to your desires when you pass away. This is no small detail. It can have a huge negative impact for your heirs if it is not completed correctly. A properly completed and witnessed designation of beneficiary form, with rare exception, could override any designation of beneficiary that you have stated in your will. It is very important for you to periodically review your records to make sure you have completed a designation of beneficiary form, and to determine whether or not you need to cancel or change your designation. This is very important in the case of divorce, legal separation, death of a family member, etc. If you have already retired, you might want to complete a new designation of beneficiary form (TSP-3) and forward it to the

TSP Service Office in New Orleans. A new form automatically supersedes any prior form that you may have completed. If you do not have a completed beneficiary form, the proceeds will be paid according to the government's order of precedence which may not line up with your desires. Don't let the government take control of dispersing your proceeds.

Bad Habit #4:

Paying off mortgages with TSP funds. We would all like to retire debt free. Having no mortgage payment is a great position to be in. You could take a lump sum withdrawal from the TSP to pay off the house. This could be a big financial mistake that could cost you thousands of dollars. Assuming a $50,000 dollar mortgage at retirement and a federal pension of $35,000, the adjusted gross income of this taxpayer is at least $85,000 dollars, if the mortgage is paid off using the TSP. TSP withdrawals are taxable income by the IRS. The difference in taxable income rates in this example is 10 percentage points (15% at $35,000 of income vs. 25% at $85,000 of income) costing this taxpayer an additional $12,500 in tax that must be paid. While the idea of no mortgage is attractive, the cost of paying it off with the TSP could be very high.

Bad Habit #5:

Neglecting to understand your TSP withdrawal options. I have found that a large percentage of government workers don't understand how the different TSP withdrawal options work. It's important to know your options, but even more critical when you retire and have to make a choice. Your money needs to be guaranteed to last a long time. There are ways to extend guaranteed income using TSP options if you understand them. Surprisingly, one choice often overlooked by many federal employees is the annuity option. The risk of outliving one's money is growing every day. Life expectancies in the US are getting longer as medical technologies advance. When

Social Security was put in place, mortality in the US was an average 63 years. Today that average lifespan is 78 and rising. Running out of money in retirement is a real possibility. The only choice available in the TSP that guarantees lifetime income is the annuity option. While not generally a good idea for all of your liquid assets, it can help in your overall income strategy. When examining the need for guaranteed income for expenses, utilizing an annuity with a Lifetime Income Benefit is an option to be considered. There are many highly rated insurance companies that offer these types of income annuities. You should consult with a licensed annuity advisor that can help you make sense of all the options available. A good annuity advisor can put together comparisons to determine if this type of annuity is in your best interest and that it will satisfy your needs.

Bad Habit #6:

Balancing your TSP allocations. Studies have shown that a federal employee who is too conservative with TSP fund allocations faces the real possibility of running out of money in retirement. As an example, if you could earn 6% in the TSP on $100,000, take out the interest and buy a 3.5% COLA on the income to counteract inflation, you would run out of TSP money in 21 years. That means if you retired at 55 you would be without TSP income at age 76. Let's look at it another way. If you lived to age 85, you may have had to continue working until age 64 to save enough TSP money to cover those extra years. Being overly aggressive with TSP allocations can be as bad, if not worse, as being too conservative. Trying to time the market through the C, S, I or Lifecycle fund can be a dangerous game. No one can predict or control the stock market. Remember 1987, 2000, 2001 and 2007? In 2008 the C fund lost 36.99%! The S fund lost 38.32%! And I fund? It lost a whopping 42.43%!! How would that effect your retirement plans if it were to repeat itself just before you retired? Harsh reminders of how a TSP account can be decimated by market downturns and unexpected global events. It is easy to understand why so many workers delayed retirement during and after these market downturns.

Bad Habit #7:

Trying to time the market. Several advisory companies/services claim to have success in timing TSP allocations and investing. Their track records are far from stellar! Fear, greed and emotion drive the markets that are impossible to accurately measure. Factor in global events such as terrorism, tsunamis, hurricanes, wars, rumors of wars, etc.; and predicting the markets become even more precarious. The only thing we know for sure about the future is that it is always uncertain. Take an assessment of your risk tolerance, time horizon and other investments before making random changes to your TSP allocations.

Glossary of Terms

1035 Exchange Section: 1035 sets out provisions for the exchange of similar (insurance related) assets without any tax consequence upon the conversion. If the exchange qualifies for like-kind exchange consideration, income taxes are deferred until the new property or asset is sold. The 1035 exchange provisions are only available for a limited type of asset which includes cash value life insurance policies and annuity contracts.

401(k) plan: A 401(k) plan is a tax-deferred defined contribution retirement plan that gives eligible employees the opportunity to defer a portion of their current compensation into the plan. Amounts that are deferred are excluded from the participant's gross income for the year of the deferral. The plan may provide for employer matching contributions and discretionary profit-sharing contributions.

403(b) plan: Tax-deferred annuity retirement plan available to employees of public schools and colleges, and certain non-profit hospitals, charitable, religious, scientific and educational organizations.

457 plan: Non-qualified deferred compensation plans available to employees of state and local governments and tax-exempt organizations.

Accelerated Death Benefits: (ADBs): Some life insurance policies make a portion of the death benefit available prior to the death of the insured. Such benefits are usually available only due to terminal illness or for long-term care situations.

Accidental Death Benefit: An Accidental Death Benefit is a rider added to an insurance policy which provides that an additional death benefit will be paid in the event death is caused by an accident. This rider is often called "double indemnity".

Account balance: Account balance, also called your accrued benefit, is the amount your 401(k) account is worth on a date that it's valued. For example, if the value of your account on December 31 is $250,000, that's your account balance. Each time your account is valued, it is likely to have a new balance.

Adjustable Rate Mortgage (ARM): An Adjustable Rate Mortgage offers an initial interest rate that is usually lower than a fixed rate, but that adjusts periodically according to market conditions and financial indices. The rate may go up and/or down, depending on economic conditions. To limit the borrower's risk, the ARM will almost always have a maximum interest rate allowed, called a "rate cap".

After-tax investments: After-tax Investments you make with income on which you have already paid income tax.

Amortization: The Amortization of a debt is its systematic repayment through installments of principal and interest. An amortization schedule is a periodic table illustrating payments, principal, interest, and outstanding balance.

Annual Percentage Rate (APR): The Annual Percentage Rate is the cost of credit expressed as a yearly rate. The APR is a means of comparing loans offered by various lenders on equal terms, taking into account interest rates, points, and other finance charges. The federal Truth-in-Lending Act requires disclosure of the APR.

Annuitant: An individual who receives payments from an annuity. The person whose life the annuity payments are measured on or determined by.

Annuity: A contract between an insurance company and an individual which generally guarantees lifetime income to the individual or whose life the contract is based in return for either a lump sum or periodic payment to the insurance company. Interest earned inside an annuity is income tax-deferred until it is paid out or withdrawn.

Asset allocation: Asset allocation is a strategy for offsetting systematic risk by investing specific percentages of your investment principal in different asset classes. For example, you might put 60% of your 401(k) portfolio in equity investments, 30% in fixed income investments, and 10% in cash equivalents. You use different asset allocation models and include different asset classes in your portfolio based on your investment objectives, your risk tolerance, and your timeframe.

Basis Points: Basis points is a term used by investment professionals to describe yields of bonds. One basis point equals one 100th of 1%, or .01%. A bond yield increase from 10.0% to 10.1% represents an increase of 10 basis points.

Bear Market: A prolonged decline in overall stock prices occurring over a period of months or even years.

Benchmark: Benchmark is a standard against which some variable is measured. A market index or average whose gains and losses reflect the changing direction of the market segment it tracks - such as large company stocks or corporate bonds - may serve as a benchmark for individual securities included in the index and mutual funds investing in those securities.

Beneficiary: The person who is designated to receive the benefits of a contract.

Beta: A statistically generated number that is used to measure the volatility of a security or mutual fund in comparison to the market as a whole.

Bid Price: The price that a buyer is willing to pay for a security or commodity.

Blue-chip Stocks: The equity issues of financially stable, well-established companies that usually have a history of being able to pay dividends in bear and bull markets.

Bond: A certificate of indebtedness issued by a government entity or a corporation, which pays a fixed cash coupon at regular intervals. The coupon payment is normally a fixed percentage of the initial investment. The face value of the bond is repaid to the investor upon maturity.

Bonding requirement: The individual(s) that are appointed to run the day-to-day operations of a qualified plan, as well as the trustee(s) and investment manager(s) must be bonded. The bond is required to provide protection to the plan against loss due to fraud, theft, forgery or dishonesty.

Brokerage window: Brokerage window is a designated brokerage account offered as an investment option in a 401(k) plan. Through a window, a plan participant is able to buy and sell individual securities and other investments. While the percentage of plans offering brokerage windows is increasing, opinion is divided on the wisdom of giving participants so wide a choice.

Bull Market: A prolonged increase in overall stock prices usually occurring over a period of months or even years.

Capital Gains Tax: Capital Gains Tax may be due when you sell taxable investments for more than you paid to buy them. The tax on long-term gains, which applies to the sale of investments you've owned more than a year, is calculated at a maximum rate of 15% and may be as low as 5%.

Capital preservation: Capital preservation is an investment strategy designed to protect the assets you have. In most cases, you choose insured investments or other products that pose little or no risk to the principal. However, in using this strategy you do expose yourself to inflation risk since you're likely to realize only a marginal increase in the value of your portfolio.

Cash Value: Permanent life insurance policies provide both a death benefit and an investment component called a Cash Value. The Cash Value earns interest and often appreciates. The policyholder may accumulate significant Cash Value over the years and, in some circumstances, "borrow" the appreciated funds without paying taxes on the borrowed gains. As long as the policy stays in force, the borrowed funds do not need to be repaid, but interest may be charged to your Cash Value account.

Certificate of Deposit (CD): A Certificate of Deposit is a low risk, often federally guaranteed investment offered by banks. A CD pays interest to investors for as long as five years. The interest rate on a CD is fixed for the duration of the CD term.

Charitable Remainder Trust (CRT): The Charitable Remainder Trust is an irrevocable trust with both charitable and non-charitable beneficiaries. The donor transfers highly appreciated assets into the trust and retains an income interest. Upon expiration of the income interest, the remainder in the trust passes to a qualified charity of the donor's choice. If properly structured, the CRT permits the donor to receive income, estate, and/or gift tax advantages. These advantages often provide for a much greater income stream to the income beneficiary than would be available outside the trust.

Co-borrower: A Co-borrower is individually or jointly obligated to repay a loan entered into with a third party. The Co-borrower may or may not share in ownership of loan collateral.

Codicil: An instrument in writing executed by a testator for adding to, altering, explaining or confirming a will previously made by the testator; executed with the same formalities as a will; and having the effect of bringing the date of the will forward to the date of codicil.

Collateral assets: Pledged as security for a loan. If the borrower defaults on payment, the lender may dispose of the property pledged as security to raise money to repay the loan.

Commission: The fee a broker or insurance agent collects for administering a trade or policy.

Commodity: A Commodity is a physical substance such as a food or a metal which investors buy or sell on a commodities exchange, usually via futures contracts.

Common Stock: A security that represents ownership in a corporation.

Compounding: The computation of interest paid using the principal plus the previously earned interest.

Conduit IRA: An individual who rolled over a total distribution from a qualified plan into an IRA can later roll over those assets into a new employer's plan. In this case the IRA has been used as a holding account (a conduit).

Conforming loan: A mortgage loan that conforms to Federal National Mortgage Association (FNMA) or Federal Home Loan Mortgage Corporation (FHLMC) guidelines. Currently, conforming first mortgages are under $275,000 ($413,000 in Alaska and Hawaii).

Consumer debt: Debt incurred for consumable or depreciating non-investment assets. Items include credit card debt, store-financed consumer purchases, car loans, and family loans that will be repaid.

Conventional mortgage: A conventional mortgage is not insured, guaranteed or funded by the Veterans Administration, the Federal Housing Administration, or Rural Economic Community Development.

Convertible Term Life Insurance: Term life insurance that can be converted to a permanent or whole life policy without evidence of insurability, is subject to time limitations.

Credit Bureau Repositories: A Credit Bureau Repository is an organization that compiles credit history information directly from lenders and creditors into credit summaries and reports. These reports are made available to lenders and creditors to assist them in gauging an individual's credit worthiness.

Critical illness insurance: Insurance protection designed to provide a lump-sum payment equal to the full value of the policy or a percentage of the policy. This depends upon the product design, to the insured/policy owner upon the diagnosis of a covered critical illness. Typical illnesses covered include heart attack, stroke, cancer, paralysis, renal failure and Alzheimer's disease. Many policies offer a partial payment for certain medical procedures such as coronary bypass surgery or angioplasty. Some policies offer a return of all premiums in the event of death of the insured, others pay the full benefit upon the insured's death.

Custodian: A financial institution, usually a bank or trust company that holds a person or company's cash and or securities in safekeeping.

Debit Cards: Debit Cards allow the cost of a purchase to be automatically deducted from the customer's bank account and credited to the merchant.

Debt Markets: The fixed income sector of the capital markets devoted to trading debt securities issued by corporations and governments.

Debt to income ratio: The ratio of a person's total monthly debt obligations compared to their total monthly resources is called their debt to income ratio. This ratio is used to evaluate a borrower's capacity to repay debts.

Decedent: The term decedent refers to a person who has died. A term life insurance featuring a decreasing death benefit. Decreasing term is well suited to provide for an obligation that decreases over the years such as a mortgage.

Deed of Trust: A document used to convey title (ownership) to a property used as collateral for a loan to a trustee pending the repayment of the loan. The equivalent of a mortgage.

Deferral: A form of tax sheltering in which all earnings are allowed to compound tax-free until they are withdrawn at a future date. Placing funds in a qualified plan, for example, triggers deductions (not all qualified plans provide for tax deductions; contributions may, however, be excluded from gross income, i.e. 401(k) plans) for the current tax year and postpones capital gains or other income taxes until the funds are withdrawn from the plan.

Deferred compensation: Income withheld by an employer and paid at some future time, usually upon retirement or termination of employment.

Defined Benefit plan: A Defined Benefit plan pays participants a specific retirement benefit that is promised (defined) in the plan document. Under a Defined Benefit plan benefits must be definitely determinable. For example, a plan that entitles a participant to a monthly pension benefit for life equal to 30 percent of monthly compensation is a Defined Benefit plan.

Defined Contribution plan: In a Defined Contribution plan, contributions are allocated to individual accounts according to a pre-determined contribution allocation. This type of plan does not promise any specific dollar benefit to a participant at retirement. Benefits received are based on amounts contributed, investment performance and vesting. The most common type of Defined Contribution plan is the 401(k) profit-sharing plan.

Deflation: A period in which the general price level of goods and services is declining.

Depreciation: Charges made against earnings to write off the cost of a fixed asset over its estimated useful life. Depreciation does not represent a cash outlay. It is a bookkeeping entry representing the decline in value of an asset over time.

Direct Deposit: A means of authorizing payment made by governments or companies to be deposited directly into a recipient's account. Used mainly for the deposit of salary, pension and interest checks.

Disability insurance: Insurance designed to replace a percentage of earned income if accident or illness prevents the beneficiary from pursuing his or her livelihood.

Disposable income: After-tax income available for spending, saving or investing.

Diversification: Spreading investment risk among a number of different securities, properties, companies, industries or geographical locations. Diversification does not assure against market loss.

Dividend Reinvestment plan (DRIP): An investment plan that allows shareholders to receive stock in lieu of cash dividends.

Dividends: A distribution of the earnings of a company to its shareholders. Dividends are "declared" by the company based on profitability and can change from time to time. There is a direct relationship between dividends paid and share value growth. The most aggressive growth companies do not pay a dividend, and the highest dividend paying companies may not experience dramatic growth.

Dollar Cost averaging: Buying a mutual fund or securities using a consistent dollar amount of money each month (or other period). More securities will be bought when prices are low, resulting in lowering the average cost per share. Dollar Cost averaging neither guarantees a profit nor eliminates the risk of losses in declining markets and you should consider your ability to continue investing through periods of market volatility and/or low prices.

Economic cycle: Economic events are often felt to repeat a regular pattern over a period of anywhere from two to eight years. This pattern of events ends to be slightly different each time, but usually has a large number of similarities to previous cycles.

Effective Tax Rate: The percentage of total income paid in federal and state income taxes.

Efficient market: The market in which all the available information has been analyzed and is reflected in the current stock price.

Employee Stock Ownership plan (ESOP): An ESOP plan allows employees to purchase stock, usually at a discount, that they can hold or sell. ESOPs offer a tax advantage for both employer and employee. The employer earns a tax deduction for contributions of stock or cash used to purchase stock for the employee. The employee pays no tax on these contributions until they are distributed.

Estate: A decedent's estate is equal to the total value of their assets as of the date of death. The estate includes all funds, personal effects, interest in business enterprises, titles to property, real estate, stocks, bonds and notes receivable.

Estate Planning: The orderly arrangement of one's financial affairs to maximize the value transferred at death to the people and institutions favored by the deceased, with minimum loss of value because of taxes and forced liquidation of assets.

Excess distributions: An individual may have to pay a 15% tax on distributions received from qualified plans in excess of $150,000 during a single year. The tax, however, does not apply to distributions due to death, distributions that are rolled over, and distributions of after-tax contributions.

Executor: The person named in a will to manage the estate of the deceased according to the terms of the will.

Face amount: The Face amount stated in a life insurance policy is the amount that will be paid upon death, or policy maturity. The Face amount of a permanent insurance policy may change with time as the cash value in the policy increases.

Family trust: An inter vivo trust established with family members as beneficiaries.

Federal Housing Administration (FHA): The Federal Housing Administration (FHA) is a government agency that sets standards for underwriting residential mortgage loans made by private lenders and insures such transactions.

Federal National Mortgage Association (FNMA or Fannie Mae): FNMA is a private corporation that acts as a secondary market investor in buying and selling mortgage loans.

Fiduciary: An individual or institution occupying a position of trust. An executor, administrator or trustee.

Financial planner: A person who helps you plan and carry out your financial future.

Fixed investment: Any investment paying a fixed interest rate such as a money market account, a certificate of deposit, a bond, a note, or a preferred stock. Fixed investment is the opposite of a variable investment.

Fixed rate mortgage: With a fixed rate mortgage your interest rate will remain the same for the entire term of the loan. Although the rate will begin slightly higher than a comparable Adjustable Rate Mortgage (ARM), the interest rate you pay can never go up for as long as you have the mortgage.

Full retirement age: Full retirement age is the age at which you qualify to collect your full Social Security benefit. It is scheduled to increase from 65 to 67 in two-month increments. For example, people born in 1942 must be 65 and 10 months to reach full retirement age.

Fund of Funds: See Life Cycle Fund definition.

Group Insurance: A form of insurance designed to insure classes of persons rather than specific individuals.

Growth stock: The common equity of a company that consistently grows significantly faster than the economy.

Guaranteed Investment Certificate (GIC): A type of debt security sold to individuals by banks and trust companies. They usually cannot be cashed before the specified redemption date, and pay interest at a fixed rate.

Guaranteed lifetime income: Guaranteed lifetime income is money paid from a pension or an annuity over your lifetime, or the combined lifetimes of you and your surviving beneficiary.

Guarantor: A third party who agrees to repay any outstanding balance on a loan if you fail to do so. A guarantor is responsible for the debt only if the principal debtor defaults on the loan.

Guardian: A person or persons named to care for minor children until they reach the age of maturity. A will is the best way to ensure that the person or persons whom you wish to have care for your minor children are legally empowered to do so in the event of your death.

Home Equity Line of Credit (HELOC): Home Equity Line of Credit allows a homeowner to borrow against the equity in their home with specific limits and terms. This is an open end loan which allows the borrower to borrow and repay funds as needed.

Home Equity Loan: Home Equity Loan is a collateralized mortgage, usually in a subordinate position, entered into by the property owner under specific terms of repayment.

Illustration: A life insurance illustration, or ledger, is a reference tool used to illustrate how a given life insurance policy underwritten by a specific insurer is expected to perform over a period of years. The insurance illustration assumes that conditions remain unchanged over the period of time that the policy is held.

Income averaging: Income averaging allows individuals who were age 50 before January 1, 1986 to pay tax on a lump sum distribution as though it had been received over a five or ten year period, rather than all at once. By using Income averaging individuals may be able to pay income tax at a more favorable rate.

Individual Retirement Account (IRA): An Individual Retirement Account is a personal savings plan that offers tax advantages to those who set aside money for retirement. Depending on the individual's circumstances, contributions to the IRA may be deductible in whole or in part. Generally, amounts in an IRA, including earnings and gains, are not taxed until distributed to the individual.

IRA rollover: An individual may withdraw, tax-free, all or part of the assets from one IRA, and reinvest them within 60 days in another IRA. A rollover of this type can occur only once in any one-year period. The one-year rule applies separately to each IRA the individual owns. An individual must roll over into another IRA the same property he/she received from the old IRA.

Inflation: A term used to describe the economic environment of rising prices and declining purchasing power.

In-force policy: An In-force life insurance policy is simply a valid policy. Generally speaking, a life insurance policy will remain in-force as long as sufficient premiums are paid, and for approximately 31 days thereafter. (See Grace Period.)

Insurability: Insurability refers to the assessment of the applicant's health and is used to gauge the level of risk the insurer would potentially take by underwriting a policy, and therefore the premium it must charge.

Insured: A life insurance policy covers the life of one or more insured individuals.

Interest Rate: The simple Interest Rate attached to the terms of a mortgage or other loan. This rate is applied to the outstanding principal owed in determining the portion of a payment attributable to interest and to principal in any given payment.

Interest rate risk: Is the uncertainty in the direction of interest rates. Changes in interest rates could lead to capital loss, or a yield less than that available to other investors, putting at risk the earnings capacity of capital.

Intestate: A term describing the legal status of a person who dies without a will.

Investment Banker: A firm that engages in the origination, under-writing, and distribution of new issues.

Investment Company: A corporation or trust whose primary purpose is to invest the funds of its shareholders.

Investment considerations: Choosing which investments are right for you will depend on a number of factors, including; your primary objectives, your time horizon and your risk tolerance.

Investment Portfolio: A term used to describe your total investment holdings.

Investment risk: The chance that the actual returns realized on an investment will differ from the expected return.

Investment strategy: The method used to select which assets to include in a portfolio and to decide when to buy and when to sell those assets.

IRA: Individual Retirement Arrangement, also known as an Individual Retirement Account

Jumbo loan: A loan that is larger than the limits set for conventional loans by the Federal National Mortgage Association (FNMA) or Federal Home Loan Mortgage Corporation (FHLMC). This limit is currently set at $300,700.

Junk Bonds: A bond that pays an unusually higher rate of return to compensate for a low credit rating.

Keogh: A Keogh is a tax deferred retirement plan for self-employed individuals and employees of unincorporated businesses. A Keogh plan is similar to an IRA but with significantly higher contribution limits.

Lien: A lien represents a claim against a property or asset for the payment of a debt. Examples include a mortgage, a tax lien, a court judgment, etc.

Life Cycle Fund: Life Cycle Fund, sometimes called a fund of funds, is a package of individual mutual funds that a fund company puts together to help investors meet their objectives without having to select a portfolio of funds on their own. Some companies offer a set of three to five separate life cycle funds, each with a different level of risk and potential for return. You can choose from among them the specific package that suits your investment style or what's appropriate for reaching your goals within the timeframe you have allowed.

Life expectancy: Life expectancy represents the average future time an individual can expect to live. Life expectancies have been increasing steadily over the past century and may continue to increase in the future. As people are living longer the cost of retirement is increasing.

Life Insurance: A contract between you and a life insurance company that specifies that the insurer will provide either a stated sum or a periodic income to your designated beneficiaries upon your death.

Life settlement: Life settlement occurs when a person who does not have a terminal or chronic illness sells his/her life insurance policy to a third party for an amount that is less than the full amount of the death benefit. The buyer becomes the new owner and/or beneficiary of the life insurance policy, pays all future premiums, and collects the entire death benefit when the insured dies. Some states regulate the purchase as a security while others may regulate it as insurance.

Liquidity: Liquidity is the measure of your ability to immediately turn assets into cash without penalty or risk of loss. Examples include a savings account, money market account, checking account, etc.

Living Wills: If you become incapacitated, this document will preserve your wishes and act as your voice in medical decisions, if you are unable to speak for yourself as a result of medical reasons.

Loan-to-value ratio: Loan-to-value ratio represents the relationship between all outstanding and proposed loans on a property and the appraised value of the property. For example, an $80,000 loan on a $100,000 property would represent an 80% loan-to-value ratio. This ratio assists a lender in determining the risk associated with the loan. The higher this ratio, the riskier the loan.

Long position: Long position in an investment indicates a current ownership in that investment which would increase in value as the underlying asset(s) increase in value, opposite of a short position.

Matching contribution: Matching contribution is money or company stock your employer adds to your 401(k) account, usually figured as a percentage of the amount you contribute. Employers are not required to match contributions, but may do so if they wish. Employers must also choose a vesting schedule that conforms to federal guidelines to determine how long you must be on the job to be entitled to transfer or withdraw the matching contributions.

Medical Power of Attorney: This special power of attorney document allows you to designate another person to make medical decisions on your behalf.

Minimum distributions: An individual must start receiving distributions from a qualified plan by April 1st of the year following the year in which he/she reaches age 70. Subsequent distributions must occur by each December 31st. The minimum distributions can be based on the life expectancy of the individual or the joint life expectancy of the individual and beneficiary.

Mortality: Mortality is the risk of death of a given person based on factors such as age, health, gender, and lifestyle.

Mortgage: A legal instrument providing a loan to the mortgagee to be used to purchase a real property in exchange for a lien against the property.

Mortgage Broker: Mortgage Broker acts as an intermediary between a borrower and a lender. A broker's expertise is to assist the borrower in identifying mortgage lenders and products that they might not identify otherwise.

Mortgage Insurance (MI): Mortgage Insurance protects the lender against the default of higher risk loans. Most lenders require mortgage insurance on loans where the loan-to-value ratio is higher than 80% (less than 20% equity).

Municipal Bonds: A bond offered by a state, county, city or other political entity (such as a school district) to raise public funds for special projects. The interest received from municipal bonds is often exempt from certain income taxes.

Mutual Funds: Mutual Fund is a pooling of investor (shareholder) assets, which is professionally managed by an investment company for the benefit of the fund's shareholders. Each fund has specific investment objectives and associated risk. Mutual funds offer shareholders the advantage of diversification and professional management in exchange for a management fee.

Net asset value: The value of all the holdings of a mutual fund, less the fund's liabilities (also describes the price at which fund shares are redeemed).

Net worth: Your net worth is the difference between your total assets and total liabilities.

Non-conforming loan: A loan that does not conform to Federal National Mortgage Association (FNMA) or Federal Home Loan Mortgage Corporation (FHLMC) guidelines. Such loans include jumbo loan, sub-prime loans and high risk loans. Also known as the type of loans that caused the mortgage crisis!

Note: Note is a legal document that acknowledges a debt and the terms and conditions agreed upon by the borrower.

Open-end fund: An Open-end mutual fund continuously issues and redeems units, so the number of units outstanding varies from day to day. Most mutual funds are open-end funds. The opposite of closed-end fund.

Origination fee: The origination fee on a mortgage is usually the amount charged by the lender for originating the loan. Origination fees vary by lender and are expressed in points where one point is equal to 1% of the original loan balance.

Over-the-counter (OTC) Market: Market created by dealer trading as opposed to the auction market, which prevails on most major exchanges.

Paper gain (loss): Unrealized capital gain (loss) on securities held in portfolio, based on a comparison of current market price to original cost.

Payroll Deduction: Payments made on your behalf by your employer. They are automatically deducted from your pay check.

Points: Points are charges added to a mortgage loan by the lender and are based on the loan amount. One point is equal to 1% of the original loan balance.

Policy: A contractual arrangement between the insurer and the insured describing the terms and conditions of the life insurance contract.

Policy loan: The policy owner can borrow from the cash value component of many permanent insurance policies for virtually any purpose. Any policy loans that are outstanding at the time of death of the insured will be deducted from the benefit paid to the beneficiary.

Power of Attorney: A legal document authorizing one person to act on behalf of another.

Premium: The payment that the owner of a life insurance policy makes to the insurer. In exchange for the premium payment, the insurer assumes the financial risk (as defined by the insurance policy) associated with the death of the insured.

Present value: The current worth of a future payment, or stream of payments, discounted at a given interest rate over a given period of time.

Pretax investments: Pretax investments are made with employment earnings subtracted from your pay before income tax is calculated and withheld. These investments, which are not reported as current income, go into a tax-deferred account. Income tax, calculated at your regular tax rate, is due on these investments and their earnings when you withdraw from that account.

Principal: The principal amount of a loan or mortgage is the outstanding balance, excluding interest.

Private mortgage insurance: Private mortgage insurance protects the lender against the default of higher risk loans. Most lenders require private mortgage insurance on loans where the loan-to-value ratio is higher than 80% (less than 20% equity).

Probate: The process used to make an orderly distribution and transfer of property from the deceased to a group of beneficiaries. The probate process is characterized by court supervision of property transfer, filing of claims against the estate by creditors and publication of a last will and testament.

Profit Sharing plan: A Profit Sharing plan is the most flexible and simplest of the defined contribution plans. It permits discretionary annual contributions that are generally allocated on the basis of compensation. The employer will determine the amount to be contributed each year depending on the cash-flow of the company. The deduction for contributions to a Profit-Sharing plan cannot be more than 15% of the compensation paid to the employees participating in the plan. Annual employer contributions to the account of a participant cannot exceed the smaller of $30,000 or 25 percent of a participant's compensation.

Prohibited IRA transactions: Generally, a prohibited transaction is any improper (self-dealing) use of the IRA by the account owner. Some examples include borrowing money from an IRA, using an IRA to secure a loan and selling property to an IRA.

Prospectus: A detailed statement prepared by an issuer and filed with the SEC prior to the sale of a new issue. The Prospectus gives detailed information on the issue and on the issuer's condition and prospects.

Qualified Retirement plan: A Qualified Retirement plan is a retirement plan that meets certain specified tax rules contained primarily in section 401(a) of the Internal Revenue Code. These rules are called plan qualification rules. If the rules are satisfied, the plan's trust is exempt from taxes.

Refinance: To refinance one's mortgage is to retire the existing mortgage using the proceeds of a new mortgage and using the same property as collateral. This is usually done to secure a lower interest rate mortgage or to access equity from the property.

Registered Representative: Registered Representative is licensed with the NASD (National Association of Securities Dealers), through association with an NASD member broker/dealer, to act as an account representative for clients and collect commission income.

Revolving Debt: A debt or liability that does not have a fixed principal balance or payment. Examples include credit cards, home equity lines of credit, etc.

Rider: A life insurance rider is an amendment to the standard policy that expands or restricts the policy's benefits. Common riders include a disability waiver of premium rider and a children's life coverage rider.

Rule of 72: A way to determine the effect of compound interest. Divide 72 by the expected return on your investment. If your expected return is 8%, assuming that all interest is reinvested, you will double your money in 9 years.

Salary Reduction Simplified Employee Pension (SARSEP): A SARSEP is a simplified alternative to a 401(k) plan. It is a SEP that includes a salary reduction arrangement. Under this special arrangement, eligible employees can elect to have the employer contribute part of their before-tax pay to their IRA. This amount is called an "elective deferral".

SEC: The main regulatory body regulating the securities industry is called the Securities and Exchange Commission.

Securities: Stocks and bonds are traditionally referred to as securities. More specifically, stocks are often referred as "equities" and bonds as "debt instruments".

Securities and Exchange Commission: The main regulatory body regulating the securities industry is called the Securities and Exchange Commission.

Simplified Employee Pension (SEP): A SEP provides employers with a "simplified" alternative to a qualified profit-sharing plan. Basically, a SEP is a written arrangement that allows an employer to make contributions towards his or her own and employees' retirement, without becoming involved in a more complex retirement plan. Under a SEP, IRAs are set up for each eligible employee. SEP contributions are made to IRAs of the participants in the plan. The employer has no control over the employee's IRA once the money is contributed.

Small Cap: A Small Cap stock is one issued by a company with less than $1.7 billion in market capitalization.

Smart Card: A card with an embedded computer chip which stores more information, performs more functions and is more secure than a credit card or debit card.

Spousal IRA: An individual can set up and contribute to an IRA for his/her spouse. This is called "Spousal IRA" and can be established if certain requirements are met. In the case of a spousal IRA, the individual and spouse must have separate IRAs. A jointly owned IRA is not permitted.

Stock: Stock certificates represent an ownership position in a corporation. Stockholders are often entitled to dividends, voting rights, and financial participation in company growth.

Stock Dividends: The investor's share of the income earned by the company issuing the stock.

Stock Exchange: A public market for trading of equities and for the buying and selling of public stocks.

Surrender value: When a policy owner surrenders his/her permanent life insurance policy to the insurance company, he or she will receive the surrender value of that policy in return. The surrender value is the cash value of the policy plus any dividend accumulations, plus the cash value of any paid-up additions minus any policy loans, interest, and applicable surrender charges.

Systematic withdrawal: Systematic Withdrawal is a plan you establish to receive income from a managed account, mutual fund, or variable annuity on a regular basis over a period of years. Systematic withdrawals are flexible, so you can change the amount if you wish. But you aren't guaranteed lifetime income.

Tax Credit: An income tax credit directly reduces the amount of income tax paid by offsetting other income tax liabilities.

Tax Deduction: A reduction of total income before the amount of income tax payable is calculated.

Tax-Deferred: The term tax-deferred refers to the deferral of income taxes on interest earnings until the interest is withdrawn from the investment. Some vehicles or products that enjoy this special tax treatment include permanent life insurance, annuities, and any investment held in IRA's.

Tax-Sheltered Annuity (TSA): Tax-deferred annuity retirement plan available to employees of public schools and colleges, and certain non-profit hospitals, charitable, religious, scientific and educational organizations.

Technical analysis: Technical analysis is a technique of estimating a stock's future value strictly by examining its prices and volume of trading over time. Technical analysis is the opposite of fundamental analysis.

Term insurance: Term insurance is life insurance coverage that pays a death benefit only if the insured dies within a specified period of time. Term policies do not have a cash value component and must be renewed periodically as dictated by the insurance contract.

Testamentary trust: A trust created under the terms of a will and that **takes effect upon the death of the testator.**

Ticker Symbol: A Ticker Symbol is a combination of letters that identifies a stock-exchange security.

Title: A legal document establishing property ownership.

Total disability: In order to make a disability claim a person must meet the definition of disability set forth in the insurance contract. There are two general definitions of disability used in today's contracts. The first definition is that the insured is unable to perform all of the substantial and material duties of his/her own occupation. The second, and more restrictive, definition is that the insured is unable to perform any occupation for which he/she is reasonably suited by education, training, or experience.

Treasury Bill: Treasury Bills, often referred to as T-bills, are short-term securities (maturities of less than one year) offered and guaranteed by the federal government. They are issued at a discount and pay their full face value at maturity.

Treasury Bonds: Treasury Bonds are issued with maturities of more than 10 years and are offered and guaranteed by the U.S. Government. They are issued at a discount and pay their full face value at maturity.

Treasury Notes: Treasury Notes are issued with maturities between one and 10 years. These notes are offered and guaranteed by the U.S. Government. They are issued at a discount and pay their full face value at maturity.

Underwriter (banking): A person, banker or group that guarantees to furnish a definite sum of money by a definite date in return for an issue of bonds or stock.

Underwriter (insurance): The one assuming a risk in return for the payment of a premium, or the person who assesses the risk and establishes premium rates.

Underwriter (investments): In the bond/stock market means a brokerage firm or group of firms that has promised to buy a new issue of bonds/shares from a government or company at a fixed discounted price, than arranges to resell them to investors at full price.

Unemployment Rate: The number of people unemployed measured as a percentage of the labor force.

Universal Life Insurance: An adjustable Universal Life Insurance policy provides both a death benefit and an investment component called a cash value. The cash value earns interest at rates dictated by the insurer. The policyholder may accumulate significant cash value over the years and, in some circumstances, "borrow" the appreciated funds without paying taxes on the borrowed gains (taxes may be required if policy is surrendered). As long as the policy stays in force the borrowed funds do not need to be repaid, but interest may be charged to your cash value account. Premiums are adjustable by the policy owner.

Variable investment: A variable investment is any investment whose value, and therefore returns, fluctuates with market conditions such as a common stock, a plot of raw land, and a hard asset.

Variable Rate Mortgage (VRM): A Variable Rate Mortgage offers an initial interest rate that is usually lower than a fixed rate, but that adjusts periodically according to market conditions and financial indices. The rate may go up and/or down, depending on economic conditions. To limit the borrower's risk, the VRM will almost always have a maximum interest rate allowed, called a "rate cap".

Variable Universal Life Insurance: A Variable Life Insurance policy provides both a death benefit and an investment component called a cash value. The owner of the policy invests the cash value in sub accounts selected by the insurer. The policyholder may accumulate significant cash value over the years and "borrow" the appreciated funds without paying taxes on the borrowed gains (taxes may be required if policy is surrendered). As long as the policy stays in force the borrowed funds do not need to be repaid, but interest may be charged to your cash value account.

Vesting: Vesting entitles you to the contributions your employer has made to a pension or retirement savings plan for you, including matching contributions to salary reduction plans. You become vested when you have been employed at that job for at least the minimum period the plan requires. Those limits are established by federal law.

Viatical settlement: Occurs when a person with terminal or chronic illness sells his/her life insurance policy to a third party for an amount that is less than the full amount of the death benefit. The buyer becomes the new owner and/or beneficiary of the life insurance policy, pays all future premiums, and collects the entire death benefit when the insured dies. Some states regulate the purchase as a security while others may regulate it as insurance.

Waiver of Premium: A Waiver of Premium rider on an insurance policy sets for conditions under which premium payments are not required to be made for a time. The most popular waiver of premium rider is the disability waiver under which the owner of the policy (also called the policyholder) is not required to make premium payments during a period of total disability.

Whole Life Insurance: A traditional Whole Life Insurance policy provides both a death benefit and a cash value component. The policy is designed to remain in force for a lifetime. Premiums stay level and the death benefit is guaranteed. Over time, the cash value of the policy grows and helps keep the premium level. Although the premiums start out significantly higher than that of a comparable term life policy, over time the level premium eventually is overtaken by the ever-increasing premium of a term policy.

Will: The most basic and necessary of estate planning tools. A Will is a legal document declaring a person's wishes regarding the disposition of their estate. A Will ensures that the right people receive the right assets at the right time. If an individual dies without a Will they are said to have died intestate.

Yield: The yield on an investment is the total proceeds paid from the investment and is calculated as a percentage of the amount invested.

Annuity Glossary

Accumulation units: The shares of ownership you have in a variable annuity investment portfolio during the period you are saving for retirement. As you pay additional premiums, you buy additional units.

Annuitant: The person who receives income from an annuity. The annuitant's life expectancy is used to figure the initial income amount the annuity pays.

Annuitize: To convert the accumulated value of an annuity into a stream of income, either for one or more life-times or a specific period of time.

Annuity contract: A legal agreement between you and an insurance company, sometimes called an annuity company.

Annuity units: The number of units you own in a variable annuity investment portfolio during the period you are taking income. The number of your annuity units is fixed, and does not change.

Assumed Interest Rate (AIR): The rate of interest an annuity provider uses in determining the amount of each variable annuity income payment. Also known as the benchmark rate or the hurdle rate.

Annuity purchase rate: The cost of an annuity based on insurance company tables, which take into account various factors such as your age and gender.

Commutable contract: An annuity contract that allows you to terminate an annuity agreement that is paying you income on a fixed period or fixed percentage basis.

Contract Value: The combined total of your principal and the portfolio earnings in a variable annuity, up to and including the date on which you annuitize. Also known as accumulate value.

Deferred annuity: An annuity contract that you purchase either with a single premium or with periodic payments to help save for retirement. With a Deferred Annuity, you can choose the point at which you convert the accumulated principal and earning in your contract to a stream of income.

Expense ratio: The amount, as a percentage of your total annuity account value that you pay annually for operating, management, and insurance expenses.

Fixed annuity: An annuity contract that guarantees you will earn a stated rate of interest during the accumulation phase of a deferred annuity, and that you will receive a fixed amount of income on a regular schedule when you annuitize.

Guaranteed Death Benefit: The assurance that your beneficiaries will receive at least the amount you put into the annuity and typically your locked-in earnings if you die before beginning to take income. This guarantee is one of the insurance benefits that annuities provide.

Immediate annuity: An annuity contract that you buy with a lump sun and begin to receive income from within a short period, always less than 13 months. An Immediate Annuity can be either fixed or variable.

Income options: The various methods of receiving annuity income that an annuity contract offers. You may choose from among them the one that suits your situation best. Typically, there are six or more choices, many guaranteeing income for life.

Investment Portfolio: A collection of individual investments chosen by a professional manger to produce a clearly defined investment objective. Portfolios, which are structured the same way as open-end mutual funds, are offered in a variable annuity contract and are available to people who purchase the contract. They also are called sub-accounts or investment account.

Market Value Adjustment: This feature, which is included in some annuity contracts, imposes an adjustment, or fee, if you surrender your fixed annuity or the fixed account of your variable annuity. The adjustment offsets any losses the insurance company might incur in liquidating assets to pay the amount due to you.

Nonqualified annuity: An annuity contract you buy individually rather than as part of an employer sponsored qualified retirement plan. You pay the premium with after-tax dollars. With a deferred nonqualified annuity, your principal grows tax deferred.

Premium: The amount you pay to buy an annuity or any other insurance product. With a single premium annuity you pay just once, but with other types you pay an initial premium and then make additional premium payments.

Principal: The amount of money you use to purchase an annuity, bond, mutual fund, stock or other investment. The Principal is the base on which your earnings accumulate.

Proprietary Portfolios: The investment portfolios offered within a variable annuity that are run by the insurance company's investment managers. The annuity may also offer portfolios run by managers working for another financial institution, such as a mutual fund.

Qualified annuity: An annuity contract you buy with pretax dollars as part of an employer-sponsored qualified retirement plan.

Rollover: An IRA or qualified retirement plan that you move from one trustee to another is known as a Rollover. You can rollover any qualified plan, including a qualified annuity, into an IRA, preserving its tax-deferred status.

Separate account: The account established by the insurance company to hold the money you contribute to your variable annuity. It is separate from the company's general account, where fixed annuity premiums are deposited. Money in the separate account is not available to the company's creditors.

Single premium annuity: This type of annuity contract is purchased with a one-time payment. All immediate annuities and some deferred nonqualified annuities are in this category.

Sub-account: The investment portfolios offered in variable annuity contracts are sometimes referred to as sub-accounts. The term refers to their position as accounts held within the separate account of the insurance company offering the variable annuity.

Tiered interest crediting: A policy used by some companies who credit different interest rates to a fixed annuity's cash surrender value than they do to its annuitize value. This means the interest rate you earn is based on whether you surrender the annuity for cash or annuitize the contract for at least a minimum period and agree to the company's rules about how and when you can access your money. Typically, the rate is significantly higher if you choose the annuitization option. When comparing contracts, it's important to know if the rate you're being quoted applies to the cash surrender value or the annuitized value.

Underlying investments: The stocks, bonds, cash equivalents or other investments purchased by a variable annuity portfolio or mutual fund with the money you and other people allocate to that portfolio or fund.

Unit Value: The dollar value of a single accumulation or annuity unit, which changes constantly to reflect the current combined total value of the underlying investments in your investment portfolios, minus expenses.

Variable annuity: An annuity contract that allows you to allocate your premium among a number of investment portfolios. Your contract value, which can fluctuate in the short term, reflects the performance of the underlying investments held in those portfolios, minus the contract expenses.

Resources

The following resources will help you make some of the crucial benefit decisions discussed throughout this book:

- **www.narfe.org** - Established in 1921, NARFE works to safeguard and improve the earned rights and benefits of America's active and retired federal employees.

- **www.federaldaily.com** - A leading provider of books, newsletters and other information services to federal employees. They also publish one of the most technical, comprehensive and informative books regarding federal benefits, *The Federal Employees Almanac*, and it is a must own for all federal employees.

- **www.usa.gov** - Obtain official information and services from the U.S. government...online! They make it easy and offer an abundance of information, services and resources.

- **www.benefitscheckup.org** - Many older people need help paying for prescription drugs, health care, utilities and other basic needs. Ironically, millions of older Americans - especially those with limited incomes - are eligible for but not receiving benefits from existing federal, state and local programs. Ranging from heating and energy assistance to prescription savings programs to income supplements, there are many public programs available to seniors in need if they only knew about them and how to apply for them. Developed and maintained by the National Council on Aging (NCOA), Benefits Check Up is the nation's most comprehensive web-based service to screen for benefits programs for seniors with limited income and resources. Benefits Check Up includes more than 1, 700 public and private benefits programs from all 50 states and the District of Columbia, such as:

- Prescription drugs
- Nutrition (including Supplemental Nutrition Assistance (SNAP)/Food Stamps)
- Energy assistance
- Financial
- Legal
- Health care
- Social Security
- Housing
- In-home services
- Tax relief
- Transportation
- Educational assistance
- Employment
- Volunteer services

Since 2001, millions of people have used Benefits Check Up to find benefits programs that help them pay for prescription drugs, health care, rent, utilities, and other needs. For more information on Benefits Check Up, contact them at comments@benefitscheckup. org.

For additional information, or to schedule a private consultation concerning your specific situation, please visit our website at www.federalemp.com and fill out the information in the contact us section.